Economies of Control

Economies of Control

How Currency, Data & Digital ID Systems Are Becoming Weapons of Rule

By

Arun Thorne

Vij Books

New Delhi (India)

Published by

Vij Books
(Publishers, Distributors & Importers)
4836/24, 3rd Floor, Ansari Road
Delhi – 110 002
Phone: 91-11-43596460
Mobile: 98110 94883
e-mail: contact@vijpublishing.com
www.vijbooks.in

ISBN: 978-81-99117-91-4 (PB)

This book was developed using advanced writing tools to support the drafting and ideation process. All content has been thoughtfully curated, refined, and reviewed to ensure quality and relevance.

Contents

Introduction

The Cage You Can't See

Control today does not arrive with boots on the ground or guns at the gate. It arrives silently, under the guise of convenience, wrapped in design that feels intuitive, and endorsed by platforms that claim to know us better than we know ourselves. We unlock our phones with our faces, move through airports without showing a passport, receive money without ever touching cash—and in the process, give away more than we realise. What looks like progress may, in fact, be permissioned dependence. What feels like empowerment may be engineered consent.

This book begins with a simple but unsettling proposition: that the modern world is not being governed merely through law, but through interface. The choices we see, the services we access, the rights we exercise—they are all increasingly mediated by technologies that do not just respond to us, but shape us. The promise of the digital age was freedom: seamlessness, personalisation, the collapse of friction. Yet friction, it turns out, had a purpose. It slowed things down. It created space for reflection, for refusal, for divergence. What happens when that space disappears?

Economies of Control is not a book about future dystopias—it is a map of the control systems already operational, embedded not in the margins of society but in its core architecture. Digital currencies that can be programmed to expire or restrict spending. Biometric identity systems that determine access to services—and to citizenship itself. Algorithmic scoring engines that assign trust, risk, and worth. These are not tools awaiting misuse. They are functioning as designed.

What unites these mechanisms is not simply their technological sophistication, but their ability to naturalise compliance. They do not impose obedience with violence; they invite it with design. A button you cannot refuse. A form you cannot skip. A feature that knows your habits better than you do. Control today is not the domination of the body—it is the conditioning of the mind. And that makes it far harder to detect, let alone resist.

This book is written at a moment when the very definitions of autonomy, freedom, and agency are being rewritten—not by new laws, but by new defaults. We are told we live in an age of individual choice, and yet our choices are increasingly predicted, nudged, and constrained by systems we cannot interrogate and did not opt into. Infrastructures once built for efficiency now govern eligibility. Decisions once made in public forums are now rendered by proprietary code. The rule of law is being quietly replaced by the rule of system.

The question at the heart of *Economies of Control* is not "What are we being forced to do?" but "What are we being trained to accept?" This is a book about the domestication of the human will—not through tyranny, but through touchscreens. Not with orders, but with dashboards. Not under threat, but under terms of service.

Throughout history, the mechanisms of power have evolved in tandem with the technologies of their time. The printing press enabled the Protestant Reformation, just as broadcast media enabled the rise of mass propaganda. But the control systems of our present era are more insidious. They do not broadcast; they personalise. They do not command; they curate. They do not punish dissent; they design it out of the interface.

To understand this new paradigm, we must turn not just to politics or economics, but to behavioural science, design theory, and the psychology of submission. We must understand how systems are built to *feel* liberating while functioning coercively. The architecture of the digital world is not neutral—it has ideology encoded into its logic, bias baked into its algorithms, and intent behind its design choices. The more seamless the experience, the less visible the cost.

Consider the biometric identity card that speeds up welfare disbursement, but excludes millions when the fingerprint reader fails. Or the digital wallet that replaces cash, but allows governments to freeze assets with a keystroke. Or the social scoring system that promises public safety, but penalises the politically inconvenient. These are not side-effects. They are features of systems designed not to serve, but to sort. And in the process, to domesticate.

It is no longer enough to ask whether a technology works. We must ask what it normalises. Who it empowers. Who it erases. And what habits it builds in those who use it. Power has migrated from institutions to infrastructures. From borders to databases. From parliaments to platforms. And it has done so largely unnoticed—because the interface was smooth, the login was easy, and the convenience was addictive.

Each chapter of this book examines a different layer of this new architecture of control. From user-friendly designs that conceal coercion, to digital ID systems that turn identity into infrastructure. From programmable money that shapes behaviour without legislation, to algorithmic governance that replaces democratic process with predictive analytics. From surveillance disguised as care, to psychological strategies that numb resistance before it can form.

This book offers no fantasy of escape. Instead, it offers something more radical: the possibility of *mental sovereignty*. The ability to see the cage—even when it is built with glass and framed in chrome. To notice where freedom has been simulated. To decode the systems shaping your sense of value, your access to rights, your understanding of self. It invites the reader not merely to critique the world, but to observe its design with sharper eyes.

The great shift of our time is not technological, but epistemological. It is about what we are allowed to know, what we are trained to ignore, and what we internalise as inevitable. A digital system does not simply record what is true—it defines what is visible. And what is visible becomes what is real. When a credit score decides your worthiness, or a predictive model forecasts your future, abstraction becomes fate.

We must resist the illusion that these systems are merely tools. Tools imply discretion, human agency, reversibility. But many of the infrastructures being built today are not tools—they are terrains. Once embedded, they define the rules of movement, of access, of legitimacy. They shape the very coordinates of existence. The danger is not just that they can be used to control—but that we will forget how to live without them.

There is still time to remember. To reassert the primacy of the human over the digital. To ask: what kind of systems dignify the individual, rather than manage them? What kind of progress preserves ambiguity, mystery, and dissent? This is not a rejection of technology, but a call to reclaim authorship over the systems that shape us. To design with care, to implement with humility, and to resist the seductive logic of optimisation for its own sake.

This book is not a warning. It is a lens. It does not urge panic, but perception. The hope it offers is not rooted in technological fixes or political promises, but in the mind's enduring capacity to observe, interpret, and choose. If we are being programmed, the first act of resistance is to notice the code.

Welcome to *Economies of Control.* May this be a guide not only to what has been built around you—but to what you are still free to rebuild within yourself.

Chapter 1

Systems That Feel Like Freedom

Freedom today does not announce itself with a constitution or a passport. It arrives with an interface. A swipe, a tap, a biometric scan. It speaks the language of access—seamless, intuitive, personalised—and it promises liberation through design. The fewer the steps, the freer the user. Or so we are led to believe. This chapter opens with a provocation: what if ease has become the most effective disguise for control? What if the systems we praise for their elegance are also the very ones shaping our behaviours, narrowing our choices, and scripting our consent?

For most people, the interface is where technology ends and freedom begins. The glowing screen, the responsive design, the illusion of choice laid out in toggles and tiles. But behind every polished user experience lies an architecture of power—one designed not only to serve, but to steer. In a world increasingly governed not by deliberation but by default, the line between convenience and coercion has blurred. We are no longer merely using technology; we are being used by it—subtly, persistently, and often willingly.

The question is no longer whether a system can be trusted, but whether its design ever gave us a real choice to begin with. When a banking app nudges you toward a "smart savings" product with embedded risk, or a social media platform silently recalibrates its privacy settings during an update, or a national ID portal links access to food rations with a successful fingerprint scan—are you making a decision, or are you being designed into one?

This chapter traces the invisible scaffolding of modern digital life, beginning with *The Interface Illusion*. Interfaces are not neutral surfaces. They are the visible masks of complex, often opaque infrastructures—systems of data collection, behavioural influence, and access control. The facial recognition gate that grants you entry to a secure building does not merely read your features; it interprets them against a database, applies thresholds of confidence, and enacts a decision made by someone—or something—

you'll never meet. The illusion is that the interaction is between you and a machine. The reality is that you are entering into a relationship with an ecosystem of assumptions, algorithms, and accountability gaps. Interfaces aestheticise control. They wrap it in the language of personalisation, efficiency, and empowerment, even as they extract value, enforce norms, and constrain possibility.

The logic of *Consent by Design* is equally subtle and pervasive. Consent is no longer about informed agreement—it is about engineered acquiescence. From India's Aadhaar system to Singapore's Smart Nation initiative, design decisions guide user behaviour in ways that feel voluntary but are, in practice, deeply coercive. Consider default settings: the seemingly minor choice of opting in or out of data sharing. Numerous studies in behavioural economics have shown that defaults shape behaviour far more than deliberation. When the default is surveillance, opting out becomes both technically arduous and socially penalising. Add gamified feedback loops—like the satisfaction of reaching a "profile completeness" score, or the dopamine rush of unlocking new features—and the system doesn't just solicit your participation; it conditions it. The platform becomes a behavioural trainer, and the user, a domesticated subject. Facebook's privacy architecture is a masterclass in such dynamics: granular enough to imply control, but labyrinthine enough to discourage real understanding. The end result is not transparency, but the theatre of choice.

The Invisible Bureaucrat takes this logic further, examining how algorithmic systems have supplanted human gatekeepers under the banner of objectivity. But these systems are not neutral. They encode priorities, biases, and exclusions in code that is rarely subject to public scrutiny. A machine learning model deciding who receives housing benefits, a facial recognition system flagging "suspicious" activity, or a predictive policing algorithm assigning risk scores—these are the new administrators of social life. Unlike their human predecessors, they do not explain themselves. They cannot be reasoned with or held accountable in traditional ways. And their biases are harder to detect because they are embedded not in rhetoric, but in training data, feature selection, and feedback loops. The result is a governance model that feels impartial but often exacerbates historical inequities. Algorithms don't have ideologies, but they inherit the worldviews of those who train them.

Then there is *Comfort as Control*. The logic of convenience has become the ideological engine of the digital economy. We are invited to give up autonomy in exchange for frictionlessness, to allow systems to remember, recommend, and decide—so we don't have to. Nowhere is this more evident than in the ecosystems built by companies like Tencent and Apple. China's WeChat app combines messaging, payments, government services, ride-hailing, and social media into a single, seamless experience. But this convenience comes at a steep cost: the unification of identity, location, financial behaviour, and social networks into one monitorable, controllable stream. Apple's Wallet offers a similar consolidation of power, albeit cloaked in a privacy-forward aesthetic. Yet, the ability to remotely disable a payment method or deny access to a digital key demonstrates how centralised control remains, even in the West. The more comfortable the system, the less visible the power it holds over the user.

These systems do not need to tell us what to do. They merely need to shape the environment in which decisions are made. And they do so with astonishing subtlety. Behavioural design, or "choice architecture," is now a foundational strategy in the creation of everything from insurance portals to immigration systems. Governments and corporations alike are adopting frameworks that draw from cognitive psychology and behavioural economics to pre-empt user behaviour. These systems don't demand obedience; they suggest, reward, and normalise it. The result is a population that complies not because it is compelled, but because it has been gently guided to see no viable alternative.

This chapter will not simply catalogue examples of interface-level coercion. It will teach the reader to *see* differently—to decode the semiotics of interface design, to detect when consent has been scripted in advance, and to question the neutrality of systems that present themselves as merely efficient. It will challenge the reader to move beyond convenience as a metric for trust, and to develop a vocabulary for critiquing digital systems not only on the basis of function, but of form, ethics, and power.

To that end, this chapter engages with systems both global and local, public and private. We will examine how Aadhaar in India, under the pretext of financial inclusion, created a gateway to exclusion for millions whose fingerprints could not be reliably scanned. We will look at Singapore's Smart Nation efforts, where citizens interact daily with sensors, ID-linked services, and facial verification checkpoints in a society often cited as a model of "benevolent technocracy." We will interrogate Facebook's interface evolution, where every privacy recalibration and notification placement subtly shifts user behaviour in ways that maximise data capture.

Each of these systems is built on a foundational premise: that good design is invisible. But when power is embedded in design, invisibility becomes a liability. To reclaim agency in the digital age, we must learn to interrogate not just what a system does, but *how* it makes us feel—and why. When a system feels natural, frictionless, or helpful, we must ask: whose interests were served in making it feel that way?

Ultimately, this chapter offers a lens into a deeper truth: that the interface is now a battleground for behavioural control. The buttons we press are not merely operational; they are directional. They lead us not just through a service, but through a set of pre-defined behaviours, permissions, and values. To use an interface today is to participate in an ideology—often without knowing what that ideology is.

The task before us, then, is not to reject technology, but to become literate in its persuasive grammar. To notice where design has replaced debate, where defaults have replaced deliberation, and where autonomy has been traded for UX. This is not the loss of freedom as we once defined it. It is the redefinition of freedom in terms dictated by those who build the systems we now depend on.

And so the question is not: *Are we free?* The question is: *Are we free to refuse the systems that make us feel free?*

The Interface Illusion

The most powerful systems of control today do not announce themselves with threats or restrictions. They arrive clothed in sleek design and seamless functionality. They offer you access, customisation, and speed. They ask you to "agree and continue," not because you understand what you're agreeing to, but because the alternative is to forfeit participation entirely. What looks like empowerment is often a well-disguised funnel. What feels intuitive is rarely neutral. The illusion is that you are in control; the reality is that you are being guided.

Every time we open a banking app, authorise a biometric scan at an airport, or link our identity to a payment gateway, we are engaging not just with a product, but with an infrastructure built to shape behaviour. The interface—what we see and touch—has become the most critical and least scrutinised layer of power in the digital age. It mediates our experience of systems that would be rejected outright if exposed in full. That rejection doesn't happen because the design conceals, abstracts, and reconfigures power into something that feels benign.

Take a standard mobile banking app. It offers convenience, customisable alerts, instant transfers, and budgeting tools that feel empowering. But behind that polished surface lies a mesh of behavioural nudges: suggestions to "round up" spending into savings accounts that funnel users into proprietary investment schemes; frictionless credit approvals that lead to long-term debt obligations; algorithmically generated insights that categorise spending habits into monetisable profiles. These are not merely features. They are intentional prompts that guide users toward decisions aligned with institutional objectives, often at odds with long-term financial wellbeing. Most users don't notice. That's the point.

What makes these systems so effective is their invisibility. Power is no longer about physical coercion or even overt mandates—it is exercised through micro-design choices that operate below the threshold of conscious attention. When a facial recognition gate at an airport scans your face without requiring you to present a passport, the process feels efficient. But the convenience masks a centralisation of biometric data, the normalisation of mass surveillance, and the delegation of identity verification to proprietary systems controlled by state-corporate partnerships. You weren't forced to comply—you were invited to glide through. And so you did.

Design has become the language through which power speaks—and it speaks in the dialect of ease. Across industries, we are seeing a consistent pattern: the more seamless the interface, the more opaque the underlying logic. Every "frictionless" experience has a cost, and it is usually paid in consent. But consent, in this context, is engineered. When default settings favour maximum data collection, when opt-outs are buried under multistep menus, when interfaces reward certain behaviours with badges, offers, or enhanced access—what appears to be voluntary participation is in fact a controlled environment with heavily suggested paths.

This is perhaps best illustrated by looking at how national identity systems are being implemented in digital form. India's Aadhaar programme, the world's largest biometric ID system, was pitched as a solution for financial inclusion and public service access. Its interface—typically a mobile or web portal—suggests simplicity: enter your number, verify with a fingerprint or iris scan, and proceed. But the reality is that Aadhaar's backend infrastructure has created systemic exclusion for those with worn fingerprints, inconsistent documentation, or limited digital literacy. When an interface is designed to be seamless for some, it often becomes a gate for others. The technology doesn't fail; it sorts.

Singapore's Smart Nation initiative takes a more polished, integrated approach. The government has partnered with tech firms to embed data collection into everyday experiences—from transport to healthcare to education. Citizens can use facial recognition at community centres, public libraries, and even lifts in government housing estates. The interfaces are intuitive and often optional—at first. Over time, however, these "opt-in" systems become the default, with those choosing manual alternatives relegated to slower, more cumbersome routes. The strategy is not to ban dissent, but to burden it with inconvenience.

The persuasive power of design lies in its ability to make you feel like you're making a choice—even when the environment has already made it for you. This is particularly true in digital platforms where personalisation is key. Facebook, for example, continually evolves its interface not simply to enhance user experience, but to deepen engagement. Subtle colour shifts, notification placements, and content surfacing are all calibrated through A/B testing to maximise time spent on the platform. The privacy dashboard, designed to reassure, presents users with controls that imply autonomy. Yet the complexity and vagueness of those settings often serve to obscure rather than illuminate. The result is performative transparency—enough to deflect criticism, but not enough to grant meaningful agency.

What we see, then, is a pattern: the aesthetics of user-friendliness serve to shield infrastructures of extraction. Whether it's the data harvested by a health app, the behavioural profiling done by a fitness tracker, or the facial scans processed by a "smart" security camera, the surface experience is designed to disarm. Most users interact with these systems as consumers, not citizens. They evaluate utility, not governance. And in doing so, they become participants in architectures of power that were never subject to collective deliberation.

The stakes are not trivial. As more services become digitally mediated, the interface becomes the front line of civic life. From applying for a job to accessing a vaccine, from entering a public building to proving one's identity during a protest—the screen determines the terms of participation. Who designed that screen? Whose values informed its logic? And who is accountable when it excludes, misleads, or harms?

It is a mistake to treat interface design as merely a question of aesthetics or usability. It is, at its core, a political technology. It encodes assumptions about who the user is, what they need, and how they should behave. It sets the boundaries of action, establishes norms, and communicates what is valued. A dropdown menu can define the limits of gender recognition. A red warning box can instil fear where none is warranted. A default setting can shape behavioural baselines for millions. These are not trivial details—they are expressions of power.

Consider the role of friction. In traditional systems, friction was often seen as a nuisance. But friction can also serve a democratic function. It slows things down. It prompts reflection. It creates room for reconsideration or refusal. In the digital environment, the drive toward seamlessness has systematically eliminated friction—not to enhance autonomy, but to expedite compliance. The fewer the clicks, the less time you have to think. When Apple Pay launches with a double tap of your phone's side button, the transaction is instantaneous—but so is the loss of any deliberative pause. The more intuitive the process, the less transparent it tends to be.

What makes the interface illusion so difficult to dismantle is that it plays on a shared desire: the desire for things to "just work." No one wants to spend ten minutes adjusting privacy sliders or questioning whether their biometric data will be retained indefinitely. The success of these systems depends on your willingness to trust the abstraction. But abstraction is a privilege. For many, the stakes of that trust are existential. A mismatched biometric scan can mean loss of rations in India. A flagged risk score can mean denial of a visa in the United States. A platform ban can mean loss of income for a digital freelancer.

This is not to say that all interface design is malicious. Many systems genuinely aim to simplify complex processes and improve user experience. But the key issue is asymmetry. Users are rarely aware of the extent to which their behaviours are being guided, categorised, or commodified. Designers, product managers, and policymakers—often under pressure to meet commercial or political KPIs—rarely build systems with adversarial thinking in mind. The result is a technological landscape where the architecture of choice is silently rigged in favour of compliance, extraction, and surveillance.

The only antidote to this condition is interface literacy—not just technical competence, but a critical awareness of how digital environments are structured and to what ends. This requires asking questions we're not trained to ask: Why does this button stand out more than the others? Why is this the only option highlighted in blue? What happens if I say no? What am I not being shown?

To navigate a world where interfaces have become arbiters of participation, we must learn to treat every touchpoint not just as a utility, but as a statement of intent. Not every design is dangerous, but every design is directional. It points you somewhere. And the question, always, is: *Whose direction are you following, and why?*

Consent by Design

Consent has always been central to legitimacy—whether in law, medicine, or governance. But in today's digital systems, consent is less about informed agreement and more about structured compliance. It doesn't emerge from meaningful deliberation; it's embedded in design—preloaded, preshaped, and predecided. The illusion of freedom rests on the premise that users actively choose what to share, accept, or decline. But those choices are increasingly framed in such a way that the outcome is already anticipated. The modern interface doesn't wait for permission—it scripts it.

Consider how quickly we scroll through terms and conditions. The language is dense, the interface encourages haste, and the stakes are veiled. The real issue isn't laziness or digital fatigue; it's that the structure of the interaction has been deliberately built to discourage resistance. Every toggle, notification, colour scheme, and default setting is the result of conscious design decisions meant to reduce friction—for the system, not the user. This is the essence of *consent by design*: the strategic arrangement of choice environments to produce predictable behaviour that appears voluntary.

Nowhere is this more evident than in the case of India's Aadhaar programme. Introduced as a digital identity platform to streamline welfare distribution, Aadhaar was framed as optional—initially. But that optionality quickly eroded as it became entangled with essential services: subsidies, pensions, school admissions, mobile SIM registration, even hospital access. Consent, in theory, remained intact. Users "agreed" to link their biometric data in exchange for access. But what does agreement mean when the alternative is exclusion from food rations or treatment? The interface may have included a checkbox, but the wider system functioned as a coercive apparatus. The policy infrastructure effectively transformed opt-in into no-option.

Critics of Aadhaar were often accused of being anti-modern or obstructive to progress. But the core concern was not about the technology itself—it was about how that technology was designed to collapse choice under the weight of necessity. In several reported cases, people died after being denied access to welfare due to fingerprint mismatches or system errors. The interface remained clean and unassuming. The consequences, however, were anything but. Aadhaar taught us that consent, when filtered through the language of efficiency, can be weaponised. It also showed that *when digital systems are positioned as neutral administrators, they often escape the scrutiny applied to more traditional forms of governance.*

Singapore's Smart Nation initiative provides a different but equally revealing case. Unlike Aadhaar, Singapore's strategy is not built around poverty relief but around digital optimisation. Citizens are nudged toward a fully integrated digital life—cashless transactions, smart transportation, digital health passports, facial recognition-enabled public services. The official language is one of empowerment and progress. The interfaces are exceptionally well-designed, sleek, and easy to use. But the deeper architecture is more instructive than the front-facing gloss. By integrating services into a centralised platform and promoting digital ID-linked systems across domains, Singapore has created a feedback loop where participation becomes obligatory through design rather than law.

The process is subtle. A service is first introduced as optional, then framed as a convenience, and eventually becomes de facto mandatory when its alternatives are withdrawn or rendered burdensome. For example, SingPass, the digital identity used to access everything from tax filings to public housing applications, now supports facial recognition logins. While older methods remain technically available, they are buried beneath more steps or marked as legacy options. Over time, user habits adapt not through force, but through attrition. The state doesn't need to demand compliance; it simply *designs* it.

What's particularly revealing in the Singaporean case is the language used in public communications. Citizens are not *required* to enrol in certain digital services; they are *invited* to enjoy enhanced convenience, faster processing, and exclusive features. The psychology is familiar: reward-based compliance. Gamified feedback loops—badges, status levels, early access—train users to associate participation with social and functional advantage. As services become increasingly tied to these digital systems, opting out begins to carry the implicit penalty of being left behind. The logic is simple: modern citizens are digital citizens. Resistance is rebranded as inefficiency.

One of the most pervasive examples of consent by design lies in Facebook's data policy framework. Unlike Aadhaar or Smart Nation, Facebook operates as a private entity. Yet its influence over social, political, and behavioural life is arguably more penetrating. Facebook does not coerce users into sharing data. It encourages them—by building choice architectures that present surveillance as service. Every "Like" button, story view, or reaction emoji is a data-capture point dressed as engagement. The interface makes sharing feel like a gesture of connection. But behind every gesture lies an algorithmic appetite trained to profile, predict, and monetise.

The platform's privacy settings are a case study in obfuscation. Rather than offering a single, transparent dashboard for users to control their data, settings are distributed across multiple menus, submenus, and flows. Each screen features default options that favour maximal sharing. The language is deliberately vague—permissions are framed in terms of "improving your experience," "personalising content," or "helping friends find you." These euphemisms work precisely because they camouflage extraction behind utility. The user is not denied choice—they're simply directed toward one through design friction. Choosing privacy becomes a labour-intensive process, and few pursue it.

This isn't manipulation in the crude sense—it's *strategic environment shaping*. Facebook has mastered the art of making the user *feel* in control while ensuring the business model remains undisturbed. Even the infamous Cambridge Analytica revelations didn't significantly alter user behaviour, because the interface remained unchanged. The emotional rewards were still in place. The cognitive load of resistance was still high. And the social incentives to stay connected remained irresistible. When the design of a system consistently results in the same behavioural outcome, despite varying inputs or scandals, the question of consent becomes academic.

It's tempting to see these examples—Aadhaar, Smart Nation, Facebook—as separate phenomena. But they share a common operating logic: control is embedded in the architecture of choice. The checkbox is there, the opt-out is technically available, and no one is *forced* to comply. But the system ensures that saying "no" becomes impractical, burdensome, or socially penalised. Consent becomes a performance—one designed to reassure regulators, pacify the user, and validate the legitimacy of extraction.

This poses a serious challenge for legal frameworks that rely on consent as a cornerstone principle. When design can shape decision-making to such a degree, is the resulting agreement still voluntary? Legal scholars have begun to acknowledge this problem, but regulatory solutions remain fragmented and often outdated. Most data protection laws treat consent as a binary—given or withheld. They rarely account for the nuances of design pressure, the influence of defaults, or the emotional triggers built into interfaces. This is not merely a compliance issue—it's a democratic one. If participation in digital systems is effectively mandatory, and if those systems are designed to engineer agreement, then traditional notions of autonomy and accountability no longer hold.

The counterargument is familiar: users benefit from these systems. They get faster services, more personalised experiences, and access to tools that improve their lives. This is not untrue. But benefit does not equal fairness, and comfort does not equal consent. A system can be useful and coercive at the same time. The key question is not whether users enjoy the interface—but whether they understand the terms under which that enjoyment is provided. And whether they can genuinely refuse those terms without unreasonable cost.

Consent by design is not inherently unethical. It can, in theory, be used to promote privacy, safety, or wellbeing. But in practice, it is overwhelmingly used to advance institutional interests—be they governmental control or commercial surveillance. The challenge is not to ban such techniques outright, but to *recognise them* as mechanisms of power. This requires interface literacy, regulatory innovation, and a cultural shift in how we define participation. It also requires moving beyond the assumption that visible choice equals real agency.

What we are witnessing is a reconfiguration of consent itself—from a relational negotiation to a one-sided protocol. The checkbox has replaced the conversation. The design pattern has supplanted the ethical question. The user has been positioned not as a decision-maker, but as a data point in a behavioural funnel. Until we begin to see consent not as a static event, but as a process shaped by context, design, and institutional logic, we will continue mistaking engineered compliance for genuine agreement.

The stakes are high. As digital systems increasingly mediate access to finance, education, healthcare, and civic life, the quality of consent becomes a proxy for the quality of freedom. And if that consent is consistently produced through design that narrows options, burdens resistance, and rewards submission, then what we are building is not a participatory digital society—it is a well-decorated cage. The first step toward escaping it is seeing it clearly. And that begins by asking a different kind of question: not *Did I agree?* but *What was I agreeing to, and on whose terms?*

The Invisible Bureaucrat

Ask most people where decisions are made in modern society, and they'll point to legislatures, boardrooms, or regulatory agencies. Few would mention a scoring model embedded in a credit app or a risk engine assessing a schoolchild's behaviour. Yet these algorithmic systems increasingly govern who receives a loan, qualifies for public housing, gets flagged by police, or lands a job interview. The old bureaucracies were slow, often inefficient, but visible. You could name the agency, meet the officer, submit an appeal. Today's systems operate behind screens, inside data centres, under the euphemism of "automation." The interface appears neutral. The decision arrives without a face. And the logic guiding it remains largely inaccessible.

The invisible bureaucrat is not a machine—it is a set of encoded judgments made by humans and then buried in statistical processes, model weights, and proprietary logic. The user interacts with a platform, not a person. But behind that interface lies a sequence of design choices: which data to collect, what features to prioritise, which outcomes to optimise for. Each of these choices reflects institutional values, commercial incentives, and historical biases. The veneer of neutrality—clean dashboards, automated recommendations, "objective" scores—conceals the fact that someone, somewhere, decided what counts as risk, merit, compliance, or eligibility.

Consider algorithmic hiring platforms. Companies now routinely use AI tools to screen CVs, rank applicants, or analyse video interviews. The promise is fairness and efficiency—algorithms won't be swayed by appearance, accent, or unconscious bias. But the training data for these systems often comes from past hiring decisions, which are themselves riddled with discriminatory patterns. If a company has historically favoured male applicants from elite universities, the model learns to associate those features with competence. The result is not fairness, but the replication of bias at scale. The human decision-maker is replaced, but the systemic inequity remains intact—now wrapped in the respectability of machine logic.

What makes this particularly insidious is the illusion of objectivity. Applicants rejected by an algorithm often have no way of knowing why. The system cites proprietary software, complex correlations, or vague suitability scores. There's no hearing, no explanation, and often no appeal. The bureaucracy hasn't disappeared; it has become a black box. Power still resides in judgment—but judgment has been relocated to systems designed to operate without scrutiny. The invisible bureaucrat doesn't get tired, doesn't argue, and doesn't admit uncertainty. It simply executes.

In public services, similar patterns are emerging. The city of Rotterdam implemented an algorithm to predict welfare fraud, using variables such as age, gender, nationality, and neighbourhood. The model flagged thousands of individuals for further scrutiny, often without clear evidence. Independent audits later revealed that many flagged individuals were immigrants or members of marginalised communities. The system had internalised historical patterns of policing and poverty—but dressed them up in the language of data-driven governance. Officials insisted the model was neutral, but the outcomes betrayed the opposite. When oversight was finally introduced, the system was suspended.

This is not just a European or American phenomenon. In India, predictive analytics are being tested to assess student performance, flag potential dropouts, and allocate educational resources. The intention may be benevolent—improving outcomes, targeting interventions—but the method risks embedding surveillance into the very act of learning. A student's future is increasingly shaped not by her teachers, but by a prediction based on her attendance patterns, household data, and exam scores. The bureaucrat of the past might have been fallible, slow, and biased—but at least you could argue with him. The algorithm doesn't listen.

What makes the invisible bureaucrat so difficult to contest is its structure of credibility. Algorithms are often presented as impartial because they are mathematical. But mathematics doesn't remove values—it codifies them. A risk assessment tool used by US courts, for instance, was found to overestimate recidivism among Black defendants compared to white ones. The tool, called COMPAS, drew on factors like family background, employment history, and prior arrests—all of which correlate with broader social inequities. The software's creators defended its methodology, but the tool's effect was clear: it disguised social prejudice as statistical probability.

The same logic can be seen in financial systems. Credit scoring agencies have expanded their models beyond traditional metrics like income or repayment history. In some countries, they now incorporate behavioural data: how often you charge your phone, how fast you type, whether you shop late at night. These proxies are treated as predictors of trustworthiness. But the data is thinly contextualised, often culturally loaded, and rarely subject to challenge. If an individual is denied a loan because their typing speed correlated with other "risky" borrowers, who decides whether that correlation is meaningful or fair? The answer is usually no one. The system optimises for outcomes—not accountability.

Defenders of these systems often argue that automation reduces administrative costs, increases consistency, and scales faster than human-led processes. These are valid points. But the critical distinction lies in *how* decisions are made—and *who* is accountable when things go wrong. In the traditional bureaucracy, power was at least legible. You knew the agency, the law, the appeals process. In algorithmic governance, responsibility is distributed across engineers, policymakers, and vendors. No one person owns the decision. The result is a vacuum of accountability, where the affected individual faces a wall of institutional silence.

Even when audit mechanisms exist, they often fall short. Many algorithms are proprietary, shielded by commercial confidentiality. Attempts to introduce transparency—such as requiring explanations or publishing decision criteria—are undermined by the complexity of the models themselves. Neural networks, for instance, can produce accurate predictions without yielding clear reasoning. This phenomenon, known as the "black box problem," raises fundamental questions about the legitimacy of opaque authority. If no one, not even the creators, can fully explain a decision, should that decision have the power to shape a person's life?

There are countercurrents. In Canada, efforts to implement Algorithmic Impact Assessments for federal technologies have introduced structured evaluations of risk, bias, and human rights implications before deployment. The European Union's AI Act proposes strict transparency requirements for high-risk systems. These are steps in the right direction—but they are playing catch-up with technologies already deeply embedded in the machinery of governance. The momentum of automation is strong, and its appeal—efficiency, scalability, predictability—is seductive.

What's urgently needed is a new vocabulary for interrogating automated systems. One that doesn't simply ask, "Does it work?" but "Who decides what working means?" The invisible bureaucrat thrives on the absence of such questions. It replaces the messiness of human discretion with the cleanliness of output—scored, ranked, filtered. But that messiness was often where justice lived. It was in the hesitation, the appeal, the moment of recognition that a life couldn't be reduced to a line item or a score. When that recognition is lost, governance becomes administration—and administration becomes silent control.

There's no question that digital systems will play a growing role in public and private decision-making. The challenge is not to eliminate automation, but to reintroduce human judgment where it matters most. That means embedding transparency not just in code, but in process. It means giving people the right to understand, challenge, and override algorithmic decisions. And it means treating algorithms not as neutral tools, but as political actors—shaped by values, making choices, and producing consequences.

The invisible bureaucrat is efficient, tireless, and scalable. But it is also blind to context, deaf to protest, and insulated from blame. It processes data, not lives. And unless we build systems that remember the difference, we will wake up governed by mechanisms that cannot be questioned, only obeyed. The true danger is not in the algorithms themselves, but in our readiness to trust them without knowing who they serve. That trust must be earned—not by the elegance of code, but by the openness of the institutions behind it.

Comfort as Control

The most effective systems of control today don't rely on force. They don't need to. They offer something far more persuasive: comfort. The smoother the interface, the fewer the steps, the faster the confirmation screen—the more likely we are to say yes without pause. It's not that people are failing to protect their autonomy; it's that the systems they engage with no longer ask them to. They make things easy. And ease has a cost.

Friction used to be a signal—of decision points, of accountability, of reflection. You had to carry cash, show ID, sign forms. These acts created a trail, but also an awareness. Now, convenience has become the gold standard in design, and friction has been recast as inefficiency. This shift isn't accidental. It reflects a deliberate reordering of values: user experience over deliberation, access over independence, speed over sovereignty. And it's not just digital platforms that benefit—states do too. Because once comfort becomes the baseline, people become less likely to ask what's behind it.

China's WeChat offers perhaps the most comprehensive example of convenience as architecture. What began as a messaging app has evolved into a full-service platform—users can pay bills, book medical appointments, order food, transfer money, sign legal documents, even interact with state services, all without leaving the app. This ecosystem offers extraordinary ease. But what it also creates is dependency. WeChat's design removes the need to look elsewhere. For many users, life online is synonymous with life on WeChat. The problem isn't just centralisation—it's enclosure. When every essential service is routed through a single platform, withdrawal becomes almost unthinkable. Choice still exists in theory, but in practice, most users would never risk opting out. The system makes itself indispensable. That's not just brand loyalty; it's structural lock-in.

The consequences go far beyond corporate dominance. The Chinese state has, over time, embedded its regulatory and surveillance capacities directly into WeChat's infrastructure. Because the platform is so tightly woven into daily routines, its surveillance functions don't feel like a separate imposition—they're ambient. When censorship is applied, it's rarely noticed in the moment. When a user's post disappears or an account is restricted, there's no official notice, no warning. The boundaries are enforced silently, and often algorithmically. This is control without confrontation. The interface remains friendly, the service responsive, the experience seamless. The user doesn't see the mechanism—only its output. And when life is this easy, who wants to question it?

Apple offers a compelling contrast—less overtly politicised, but structurally similar. With Apple Wallet, the company has built a platform that simplifies payments, access, authentication, and now, with digital IDs, even identification. Users can store payment cards, loyalty passes, boarding passes, and government-issued credentials in a single, unified system. The selling point is convenience, and for most users, that promise is delivered. But again, it is convenience on Apple's terms. Apple controls what kinds of cards are accepted, how they are stored, and under what conditions they can be remotely disabled. When Apple Pay launched in Russia, the company was able to suspend service in response to geopolitical developments. For users dependent on the system for daily transactions, the suspension wasn't just inconvenient—it was disabling. Their financial autonomy was suddenly contingent on decisions made in Cupertino.

The point here is not that Apple is a uniquely malevolent actor, nor that WeChat users are complicit in authoritarianism. It's that *convenience systems, by design, condition dependency*. Once a service integrates itself into multiple layers of daily life, opting out becomes more than a technical inconvenience—it becomes a form of social or economic self-exclusion. And the more indispensable the system, the more quietly control can be exerted through it.

What makes this dynamic especially effective is that it's rarely experienced as coercion. Users are not being surveilled against their will—they're being assisted. They're not being forced into a closed ecosystem—they're being offered the most elegant one. And because they opted in—through a fingerprint, a scan, a click—they often feel complicit in their own containment. The comfort flattens resistance. It dulls curiosity. It replaces the question *"Is this right?"* with *"Does this work?"*

Design choices play a critical role here. Systems that emphasise ease of use often remove the very signals that would alert users to what's being surrendered. There's no need to read terms when the default settings already allow data sharing. There's no moment of pause when a digital ID is scanned automatically. The removal of friction is also the removal of visibility. And when people can't see what's being taken from them, they can't object to it. Comfort, in this sense, becomes a buffer against scrutiny.

Even those who recognise these dynamics often underestimate their long-term impact. Dependency, once entrenched, reshapes norms. What begins as convenience soon becomes expectation, and then infrastructure. When mobile payments become the norm, those without smartphones are marginalised—not by policy, but by design. When public transport systems go cashless, the unbanked are functionally excluded. The system hasn't banned them; it has simply made their presence incompatible. That's how soft exclusion works. No confrontation, no decree—just a quiet reconfiguration of what is considered normal.

What's particularly difficult about pushing back against this is that there's no clear villain. Most people want things to be easier. Most systems are, on the surface, helpful. And in a world saturated with complexity, few are inclined to reject simplification. But it's precisely that inclination that makes these systems so powerful. They don't need to force obedience—they just need to offer an alternative that's slightly more appealing than the next. Over time, that appeal becomes infrastructure. And infrastructure becomes authority.

This is not a call to romanticise inefficiency. There's no inherent virtue in friction or analogue systems. But *when ease becomes the primary design goal, other values are often sacrificed without notice—privacy, portability, deliberation, resilience.* The question is not whether convenience is bad, but whether it is being used to shortcut autonomy. Are we choosing what works best for us—or are we accepting what's easiest because the harder option has been quietly removed?

The answer often depends on visibility. In many Western liberal democracies, systems like Apple Wallet are adopted voluntarily, with alternatives available—at least for now. In other contexts, like China, the convergence of state authority and platform design narrows those alternatives far more quickly. But the mechanisms of dependency are structurally similar: centralised platforms, default integration, and behavioural incentives that reward continued participation. What differs is the explicitness of control, not its presence.

A useful way to think about this is through the lens of reversibility. If a system collapses, or if a user chooses to leave it, how much of their life becomes inaccessible? Can they transact, identify themselves, travel, or receive services through other means? Or have the alternatives atrophied to the point of obsolescence? True autonomy isn't the absence of systems—it's the presence of meaningful alternatives. And *when convenience becomes a substitute for infrastructure, those alternatives disappear quietly, without debate.*

The risk is that we wake up one day and realise that we have built dependencies so deep they no longer feel optional. That the platforms we once adopted because they were helpful have become the conditions of participation. That the services we trusted for speed and ease now dictate the terms of our access. Control doesn't always announce itself with restrictions. Sometimes, it simply offers to make life easier—one integration at a time. And by the time we notice what's been traded away, the process is complete. There's nothing left to opt out of. Because opting out would mean opting out of life itself.

Chapter 2

The Anatomy of Digital Obedience

Obedience today is not demanded—it is designed. This chapter begins with that premise. Across societies, platforms, and institutions, we are witnessing the steady evolution of how power is exercised—not through visible coercion, but through embedded architectures that shape what we see, how we act, and who we become. The mechanics of control have become more subtle, more efficient, and significantly harder to question. They no longer rely on orders, punishments, or surveillance towers. They reside in prompts, scores, nudges, and systems that present themselves as helpful. What emerges is not less power, but a more insidious form of it: power that doesn't feel like power at all.

To understand this shift, it's useful to recall how discipline once functioned. Historically, social order was maintained through rules, consequences, and institutions—the school, the prison, the military, the hospital. These were physical spaces designed to observe, correct, and standardise individuals. But today, the discipline is ambient. It operates through design patterns in software, recommendation engines, authentication protocols, and credit algorithms. The interface has replaced the institution. Where laws once enforced behaviour, design now orchestrates it.

What's important is not just that this control is digital, but that it is seamless. The less friction we feel, the more effective the obedience becomes. When a public benefits portal guides applicants through a series of seemingly neutral steps—each decision nudged by pre-selected options, each screen suggesting what is "normal" or "recommended"—the outcome may feel chosen. But that feeling is often the product of careful design, not free deliberation. This is not conspiracy. It's craft. A craft that merges behavioural science with interface design to optimise compliance without confrontation.

This chapter unpacks the anatomy of that craft. It explores how digital systems are now used to achieve what physical discipline once could not—automated conformity at scale, masked by user experience. The sections that follow build a composite picture of digital obedience: how it is manufactured, where it resides, and why it matters. The goal is not just to critique these systems, but to understand their mechanics with enough clarity that they can be recognised, interrogated, and, where necessary, refused.

We begin by reframing control itself. *From Discipline to Design* introduces the reader to how design principles—once confined to aesthetics and usability—are now primary tools of governance. The traditional top-down model of rules enforced by law is increasingly giving way to an interface-based model of rules enforced by affordances and constraints. What you cannot click, what you are defaulted into, what behaviour is rewarded with convenience—these are the new levers of behavioural management. Unlike traditional discipline, which relied on institutional authority, digital obedience leverages habits, data, and feedback loops to influence decisions before users even realise a choice has been made.

Consider how biometric authentication is now embedded into everything from unlocking devices to accessing government services. These systems appear to offer frictionless access, but their deeper logic is exclusionary. When *identity becomes infrastructure*, the self is no longer something one declares; it becomes something one must *prove*, continuously and often invisibly. Your face, fingerprint, or iris becomes not just a key, but a condition of existence within a system. Nigeria's National Identification Number (NIN) system, for example, was introduced to streamline national databases and improve service delivery. But its rollout has systematically disadvantaged those in rural areas, the elderly, and the undocumented. In practice, access to rights and services is now contingent on successful biometric enrolment—yet failure to comply is treated as individual error, not systemic fault. The ID infrastructure has become a sorting mechanism: those who can conform to its requirements gain inclusion; those who can't are treated as invisible.

By contrast, Estonia's e-ID programme is often celebrated as a model of digital citizenship. It allows access to nearly all government services online, with transparency and user control at the forefront. Yet even in this system, the ID is more than a tool—it is a gatekeeper. Once identity becomes a programmable credential, inclusion becomes conditional, and data becomes destiny. The system defines the person, not the other way around. And while Estonia's model is built on trust and openness, the infrastructure it represents—digital identity as foundational to life—can be repurposed with very different political ends elsewhere.

These infrastructures are then linked to systems that score, rank, and sort individuals. In *The Tyranny of the Score*, we see how numerical representations of character—reputation, creditworthiness, behavioural risk—are increasingly used to govern access to opportunity. These scores may be generated by governments, as in China's social credit system, or by private actors, as in the case of credit rating agencies, ride-sharing platforms, or employment screening tools. The mechanism is consistent: reduce complex human traits to quantifiable proxies, then use those proxies to make decisions at scale. A good score unlocks ease; a bad score invites scrutiny. Over time, numbers stop reflecting behaviour—they *define* it.

The danger lies not just in how scores are calculated, but in how they reshape behaviour. When people know they are being rated, they modify their actions accordingly. This isn't speculative. In cities where social credit trials have been conducted, citizens have reported altering their online activity, refraining from political criticism, or avoiding certain associates—all to preserve or improve their score. In the United States, predictive policing algorithms assign risk scores to individuals based on prior arrests, location data, and social ties. Those flagged are more likely to be stopped, questioned, or surveilled—even if no crime has occurred. The score becomes a prophecy. And when systems are automated, those prophecies are rarely questioned. The output is mistaken for truth.

But the most dangerous feature of digital obedience is its *normalisation.* Once a control system is embedded into everyday life, it quickly becomes background noise. What initially provokes concern—the rollout of a new surveillance feature, the introduction of biometric voting, the use of predictive analytics in school admissions—soon fades into routine. In *Normalisation and the Numb*, we examine how this process unfolds, and why sustained resistance is so difficult. Humans adapt quickly. Once a practice is embedded into habit and framed as common sense, outrage has nowhere to attach itself. The system doesn't feel like control; it feels like context. Like something that just *is*.

There's a psychological dimension to this. When every transaction, application, or movement is mediated by systems that assess and evaluate, people internalise a new social logic. They learn to pre-empt the system—to adjust behaviour in advance of the algorithmic gaze. This is not obedience in the traditional sense; it's self-regulation. And it's precisely this internalisation that makes digital obedience so effective. People are not just complying with systems—they are aligning their sense of identity, possibility, and morality with them. Over time, the system no longer needs to exert pressure.

The user has already done the work.

What this chapter ultimately argues is that digital obedience is not about submission to authority—it is about calibration to systems. It is not enforced through fear, but through habit. And it is rarely noticed because it is experienced as efficiency, safety, or convenience. That's what makes it so effective. The more a control system aligns with user expectations, the less it feels like control at all. It becomes invisible, ambient, structural.

The task, then, is to make these systems visible again—not to oppose all forms of automation or optimisation, but to scrutinise *how* they are used, *who* they benefit, and *what* they assume. This chapter offers the conceptual tools to do exactly that. It shows where design replaces law, where credentials displace personhood, where scores become moral judgments, and where normalisation sedates resistance. It names the architecture so that readers can begin to see it. And it does so not to provoke despair, but to renew the possibility of agency—agency that begins with awareness, and matures through discernment.

Because obedience that doesn't feel like obedience is still obedience. And systems that are invisible are not neutral. They are simply unexamined. This chapter aims to change that.

From Discipline to Design

There was a time when control was exercised through architecture, schedules, and surveillance—through systems that trained people to conform visibly and physically. Today, it's not your posture, your punctuality, or your presence that's being shaped. It's your clicks, your taps, your default settings. What was once the domain of policy and punishment is now governed by interface. The modern user is not disciplined by institutions but by design environments that orchestrate behaviour so elegantly that resistance rarely occurs to them.

At the core of this shift is a subtle but profound transformation: the migration of control from rules to user experience, from laws to layout, from enforced obedience to behavioural guidance. What matters now is not that people follow orders, but that they move through systems in predictable, programmable ways—often without realising they are being guided at all. This is where the work of designers, engineers, and behavioural scientists converges to become the new administrators of compliance. Not with authority, but with usability.

You can see this shift in how digital services frame our interactions. A navigation app suggests the fastest route and discourages detours. A form autofills your previous answers, gently steering you to confirm them. A subscription screen makes "Accept" a bright green button, while "Decline" is greyed out, tucked in the corner. Each decision point is pre-shaped, its outcomes nudged not by mandates, but by ergonomics. Users are not required to conform—but the environment makes it easier than considering alternatives. That, in itself, is the point. *Control has become ergonomic.*

The rise of behavioural design as a governance strategy—whether in tech companies, welfare systems, or policy interventions—marks the institutionalisation of these techniques. The now-famous "nudge" theory popularised in economic policy was never limited to public health posters or default pension enrolment. It became foundational in digital experience architecture. Today's most successful platforms—from financial services to dating apps—aren't just designed to serve users. They're designed to shape their behaviour toward predetermined outcomes: more clicks, more time, more data, more transactions.

This is not merely about efficiency. It's about managing conduct at scale—without having to explicitly demand anything. Amazon's "Buy Now" button, which bypasses the shopping cart entirely, is not just a feature. It's an instruction masquerading as convenience. The button is the command. When Google Maps recalibrates your route after a wrong turn, it doesn't ask for confirmation—it assumes correction is what you want. These systems rarely need to explain themselves. They're designed to feel right. That feeling is often mistaken for freedom.

Design replaces deliberation with flow. The fewer the pauses, the smoother the interaction, the more likely users are to move through the system as intended. This is what makes behavioural control through design so effective—it doesn't obstruct the user; it ushers them along. There is no confrontation, no imposition, just a narrowing of possible actions through what is shown, what is hidden, and what is made inconvenient. When a system only highlights one path, it becomes the path of least resistance, which in practice becomes the default behaviour.

Consider the case of digital service portals run by governments. In the UK, the GOV.UK interface has become a model for streamlined public access—taxes, benefits, passports, voting. The layout is clear, the language stripped of jargon. But the structure of each form determines what counts as acceptable information, which answers are valid, and how much context the user is allowed to provide. Behind the interface is a logic of standardisation and automation. These systems don't ask what your circumstances are. They ask how well you fit the categories that have been predefined. If you don't, the form simply doesn't proceed.

This logic intensifies in systems that incorporate biometric verification or algorithmic scoring. A student loan application that requires facial verification at login, a benefits portal that cross-checks your data with predictive fraud models, or a smart thermostat that penalises manual adjustments in favour of "energy-saving modes"—all of these systems implement behavioural constraints while giving the user the illusion of autonomy. The control is not in what you are *told* to do, but in what the system *makes easy*, *makes invisible*, or *makes irrelevant*.

Design becomes especially potent when combined with habit. Interfaces train users. Repetition sets expectations. Once people become accustomed to scanning a fingerprint to open a door or waving a phone to board a train, those actions cease to feel like security procedures or data exchanges—they become routine. The habit dissolves the scrutiny. That's the moment when control is no longer experienced as control. It becomes second nature.

This has consequences for how people understand their agency. When design eliminates friction, it also eliminates the signal that something important is happening. If accepting a new terms-of-service agreement feels no different than swiping away a weather notification, how can the user be expected to treat it with deliberation? When systems are built for speed and flow, contemplation becomes an anomaly. Users are left with no cues that they're being asked to consent, decide, or comply. The design flattens the weight of the decision. *Obedience doesn't feel like obedience if it arrives in the same package as convenience.*

The troubling part is not that these systems are built to influence behaviour. Influence is a feature of all design. It's that they operate without transparency, often without recourse, and increasingly in domains where public oversight was once considered non-negotiable. In democratic societies, rules are meant to be debated, enforced visibly, and challenged if unjust. Design, on the other hand, often escapes scrutiny. It is seen as technical, apolitical, even aesthetic. But design is never neutral. Every prompt, default, and screen layout is a decision about what kinds of user behaviour are desired, tolerated, or excluded. And those decisions increasingly shape how people interact with everything from public services to financial institutions.

What we are witnessing is not a crisis of authority, but its displacement. Design now governs not only what users *can* do, but what they are *likely* to do. That probability becomes the design brief. And over time, probability begins to replace deliberation. Why ask what people *should* do when the system can model what they *will* do—and optimise for that? This shift reshapes governance itself. The regulator becomes the product team. The law becomes the interface.

This is where ethical tension sharpens. When public services adopt nudging interfaces, or when private platforms become default gateways to government functions—as in the case of digital identity systems in India or Estonia—the boundary between user experience and civic control dissolves. A well-designed prompt in a welfare app may be more powerful in shaping recipient behaviour than an actual policy change. And because it looks like usability, not authority, it avoids the scrutiny reserved for political interventions.

That's the central danger: design as a form of silent norm-setting. Not through explicit prohibition, but through alignment. Through what is visible and what is not. Through what is made easy and what is made hard. Through what is reinforced by feedback and what is allowed to fail. Design doesn't eliminate power. It redistributes it—quietly, invisibly, and often irrevocably.

To understand this shift is not to reject design, but to demand a higher standard of accountability for it. We need to stop treating user interfaces as surfaces and start understanding them as systems of governance. We need to ask: *Who set the defaults? Who benefits from the recommended action? What is being made easy, and what is being made impossible?* These are not technical questions. They are political ones.

When control is embedded in design, freedom becomes inseparable from interface. And unless we learn to read those interfaces with the same critical lens once reserved for institutions and laws, we will continue to confuse ease with consent, and usability with justice. The challenge isn't to make design apolitical—it's to make it legible. Because if obedience is being manufactured through design, then resistance will depend not on protest alone, but on perception. And perception begins with seeing the rules that have been hidden in the layout.

When Identity Becomes Infrastructure

Identity used to be something we carried—a passport, a birth certificate, a national ID card. Today, increasingly, it is something we inhabit inside systems. It is persistent, interoperable, and constantly verified. You are not simply known by your name or photograph, but by a digital credential embedded in the backend of state and corporate infrastructure. That credential isn't static. It evolves. It updates. It connects to other datasets. And most critically, it governs access. Not just to services, but to recognition itself. Once identity becomes infrastructure, it no longer merely proves who you are—it decides what you can do.

This shift, from document to digital layer, represents more than just technological modernisation. It redefines what it means to participate in society. When identity systems are made digital, biometric, and programmable, they move from being proofs of existence to preconditions for inclusion. They become not only administrative tools, but gatekeeping mechanisms. In the process, they introduce new forms of exclusion—harder to detect, harder to contest, and far more deeply embedded in everyday systems of life.

Consider Nigeria's National Identification Number (NIN), which has become one of the most ambitious digital ID initiatives on the African continent. Officially launched to streamline citizen databases and reduce fraud in public spending, the NIN system aims to register every Nigerian citizen and resident with a unique identifier linked to biometric data—fingerprints, facial images, and other personal details. In theory, it is about efficiency, accountability, and service integration. In practice, it has revealed the fragility of making digital credentials the condition for legal visibility.

Nigerians without a NIN have found themselves locked out of essential services: SIM card registration, voter enrolment, banking, pension access, and university admissions. Government messaging has consistently emphasised the urgency of compliance, with deadlines and disconnection threats. But millions remain unregistered—not by choice, but because the infrastructure simply hasn't reached them. Biometric equipment malfunctions. Rural connectivity is patchy. Names are misspelled in databases. Dates of birth are inconsistent with legacy records. These errors don't just delay access; they deny it. And when access is denied, the system itself rarely assumes responsibility. The burden of proof shifts to the individual—an individual who now lacks the very credential required to challenge their exclusion.

This is the paradox of digital inclusion through identity: the very systems meant to bring marginalised populations into visibility often become new mechanisms of marginalisation. A person without a digital ID is not just underserved—they are increasingly treated as non-existent. Paper documents are no longer accepted. Manual processing is phased out. Help desks refer citizens back to online portals. Bureaucracy becomes circular. *To fix a problem, you need the ID. But the problem is that you don't have the ID.*

What makes this shift especially difficult to challenge is that it is often framed as progress. Digital identity is positioned as a public good, a foundational building block for everything from universal healthcare to financial inclusion. And indeed, in many contexts, it has enabled meaningful improvements in access and efficiency. But progress for some can mask precarity for others. When identity becomes a prerequisite for living a connected life, any failure in that system is not a minor inconvenience—it is a structural disenfranchisement. The system doesn't say no. It simply doesn't see you.

Contrast this with Estonia, often lauded as the gold standard of digital governance. The country's e-ID system offers residents secure access to nearly every state service: voting, healthcare, taxation, education, business registration. The infrastructure is interoperable, transparent, and supported by a robust legal framework. Citizens can see who has accessed their data. They can sign documents with legal weight using their mobile devices. It is a model of what digital identity can achieve when built with trust and user control at its core.

But even here, identity is infrastructure—and that infrastructure is decisive. Opting out of Estonia's e-ID system is technically possible, but practically unfeasible. Public services are designed around digital credentials. Analogue alternatives are disappearing. If a person were to refuse the e-ID on principle or fall through its cracks for technical reasons, they would encounter enormous friction—if not outright exclusion. Estonia's model shows the best of what digital identity can be. But it also illustrates how total integration, even when well-intentioned and user-centric, can become a form of dependency that erodes alternative forms of participation.

The broader issue is not whether digital identity is good or bad. It is that once identity becomes *infrastructure*, it stops being optional. It becomes the connective tissue of everything else. And when that tissue is owned, maintained, or influenced by a small set of actors—whether states, vendors, or multilateral consortia—the risks to autonomy and agency grow exponentially. The architecture is invisible, but the stakes are enormous. Your ability to move, to work, to speak, to claim rights—each one becomes conditional on whether the system recognises you as valid.

This recognition is not always stable. Biometric systems have known error rates. Facial recognition performs less accurately on darker skin tones and female faces. Fingerprints wear with age and labour. Name formats don't always translate across cultural conventions. When identity systems are designed with narrow assumptions, they encode exclusion at the level of structure. And because the system assumes its own infallibility, those who fall outside its thresholds are treated as suspicious, anomalous, or fraudulent—rather than as people the system failed to accommodate.

Another critical issue is data centralisation. When identity becomes the point of connection between databases—medical, financial, criminal, educational—it becomes the ultimate vulnerability. A compromised identity is no longer just a privacy breach. It is an existential risk. The person whose ID is stolen may be denied benefits, wrongly arrested, blacklisted from employment, or algorithmically scored as high-risk. Recovery is rarely straightforward. The burden falls again on the individual, navigating systems that were never designed to support error correction at scale.

There is also a geopolitical dimension. Identity infrastructure is increasingly shaped by international partnerships, donor-driven development programmes, and private contractors. This can create tension between the stated goals of national sovereignty and the operational realities of transnational governance. In Nigeria, for example, aspects of the NIN programme have been supported by international funding and implemented through foreign-built systems. Questions remain about long-term data custody, cross-border data flows, and the influence of external actors on national identity regimes. Identity is presented as a domestic issue. But the pipes, protocols, and platforms often have global fingerprints.

What emerges from this analysis is not a wholesale rejection of digital identity—but a demand for vigilance. *When identity becomes the gate through which all rights and services must pass, it must be held to the highest standard—not only of accuracy and efficiency, but of justice, reversibility, and democratic oversight.* That standard is not currently being met in most systems.

We must ask: Who defines identity? Who owns it? Who can revoke it? And when the system fails—as all systems eventually do—what recourse does the individual have? Identity as infrastructure has the power to uplift or to exclude. It can enable mobility or it can harden borders. It can integrate or isolate. And the difference lies not in the interface, but in the values encoded in the architecture beneath it.

The push toward digital identity is accelerating. International frameworks, financial incentives, and technological enthusiasm are all aligned. But the consequences of getting it wrong are too severe to be treated as secondary. Inclusion cannot be presumed from adoption. Equity cannot be inferred from efficiency. And access must not be traded for conformity.

A society that builds its most fundamental systems on identity credentials must ensure those credentials are accessible, corrigible, and accountable. Because once identity becomes infrastructure, it no longer belongs solely to the person it represents. It belongs to the system. And unless that system is built with exceptional care, transparency, and humility, it will inevitably misrecognise the people who need it most.

The Tyranny of the Score

There was a time when judgement was voiced by individuals—employers, landlords, bank managers—who, for better or worse, had to stand behind their decisions. Today, those judgements are increasingly made by numbers. A credit score determines whether you qualify for a loan. A risk score decides if you're pulled aside at the airport. A trust rating from an app user influences your prospects on a platform. What was once a subjective assessment is now rendered as a quantified verdict. But these scores don't just reflect behaviour—they prescribe it. And in doing so, they are reshaping the moral architecture of daily life.

Scores promise objectivity. That is their appeal. Numbers feel neutral, immune to bias, insulated from emotion. But this neutrality is often an illusion. Every score is a model, and every model contains assumptions—about what matters, what counts, and what kind of person is considered desirable. The tyranny lies not in the existence of metrics, but in the power they've quietly accumulated. To live in a world governed by scores is to inhabit a system where your worth is constantly assessed, calculated, and operationalised—often without your knowledge, and almost always without your consent.

Few examples illustrate this dynamic more starkly than China's social credit initiatives. Frequently misunderstood as a single monolithic programme, social credit in China is in fact a patchwork of public and private systems—some run by municipal governments, others by platforms like Alibaba's Ant Group. Together, they serve as a behavioural scaffolding for both individuals and businesses. Points are awarded for actions deemed socially responsible: repaying debts, donating to charity, complying with regulations. Penalties apply for offences ranging from traffic violations to spreading misinformation online. The system is integrated into everyday life: buy baby products and your score goes up (signalling responsibility); buy too many video games and it may go down (suggesting indolence). A high score can fast-track bureaucratic processes, offer preferential access to loans, or enhance dating prospects. A low score can restrict travel, freeze assets, or publicly name and shame.

Critics rightly focus on the authoritarian potential of such systems. But the more unsettling reality is how seamlessly they are accepted—especially when participation feels rewarded. The problem is not that China invented scoring. It's that scoring is already everywhere, simply less coordinated, and less visible. In the West, scores are fragmented, commercialised, and often outsourced. Yet they serve the same purpose: filtering access, guiding behaviour, and reducing complexity into a single, decisive metric.

Take the American credit scoring system. It is one of the most consequential forms of social sorting in the country. Your score affects your ability to rent a flat, buy a car, secure insurance, or land a job. Yet few people understand exactly how it is calculated. Scores are influenced not just by how much debt you carry, but by the *type* of credit used, the *length* of your history, the *frequency* of your inquiries. Miss a utility payment and it may go unrecorded. Miss a credit card payment and your score can drop precipitously. The system is not just opaque—it is unforgiving. Errors are common. Rectifying them can take months. Meanwhile, your opportunities contract. The number becomes your reputation.

What links China's model and America's is not politics but logic. Both systems function as mechanisms of behavioural governance. They reward conformity, punish deviation, and present their outputs as factual. The score becomes a stand-in for trustworthiness, responsibility, even character. But this translation is neither accurate nor benign. It turns complex human lives into risk profiles, personal setbacks into liabilities, and social context into irrelevant noise.

Nowhere is this logic more fraught than in predictive policing. In cities across the United States, algorithms are used to forecast crime risk—at both the neighbourhood and individual level. Tools like PredPol analyse historical arrest data to identify "hot spots" for future policing. Others, such as COMPAS (Correctional Offender Management Profiling for Alternative Sanctions), generate risk scores for defendants during sentencing. These systems claim to help allocate resources more efficiently and reduce recidivism. But studies have shown that they often reinforce racial bias, penalise poverty, and perpetuate over-policing in marginalised communities.

The danger is not just that these tools are inaccurate. It's that they are used as if they are not. Judges may rely on risk scores without understanding their inputs. Police may patrol based on data that reflects enforcement patterns rather than crime itself. Individuals are flagged not because of what they've done, but because of what others like them have done. The score, in effect, becomes pre-crime. And once labelled, the person faces intensified scrutiny, reduced opportunity, and diminished recourse. The algorithm doesn't just predict the future—it shapes it.

A similar phenomenon occurs in employment screening. Platforms now scrape social media to assess candidates' online reputations. AI-driven tools evaluate video interviews for tone, posture, and facial expressions. The goal is to quantify "fit," but the outcome is often the codification of bias. Applicants are filtered not only by skills or experience, but by how well they perform according to opaque behavioural models. Those who don't conform to algorithmic expectations are silently passed over. No feedback, no appeal, just absence.

Even in contexts that appear voluntary, scoring exerts quiet pressure. On platforms like Uber or Airbnb, reputation systems play a central role in mediating trust. Drivers and hosts must maintain high ratings to remain active. Riders and guests curate their behaviour to avoid bad reviews. This creates a loop of performance and surveillance: everyone is always rating, and always being rated. The platform may present this as mutual accountability, but the asymmetry is clear. Those with lower ratings are penalised or deplatformed, often with no clear path to recovery. Reputation becomes a soft form of employment law, unregulated and unchecked.

What makes this model so resilient is that it appears efficient. Scores simplify complexity. They reduce risk. They offer a veneer of objectivity in environments marked by uncertainty. But the costs are substantial. When numbers become proxies for character, people learn to perform for the score. They self-censor, self-optimise, and second-guess. This is not paranoia—it is strategy. In a scored world, everyone is managing their metrics. And those who can't, or won't, are gradually sidelined.

More than any single example, it is this internalisation that defines the tyranny of the score. The system does not need to enforce behaviour. It teaches individuals to monitor themselves. To comply not because they are told to, but because their future depends on it. A number becomes the gateway to trust, and trust becomes conditional. The result is a moral economy where the rules are not debated, but embedded in code. And the metrics that shape us are rarely up for public scrutiny.

This is not an argument against data or accountability. Scores, when transparent, contextual, and proportionate, can serve legitimate functions. But most current systems fail on all three counts. They obscure their logic.

They strip away nuance. And they wield outsized influence over people's lives with minimal oversight. The issue is not that we measure—it's *what* we measure, *how* we measure, and *why* those measurements have been given such unassailable authority.

To live under the tyranny of the score is to inhabit a world where judgement is ambient, continuous, and often invisible. Where trust is no longer earned through relationships, but calculated through pattern recognition. Where systems reward predictability and punish deviation. And where moral standing is no longer a matter of character or conduct, but of compliance with metrics whose origins remain hidden.

We must begin to treat scoring systems not as technical conveniences, but as instruments of power. Power that decides who is trusted, who is allowed, who is desirable. And power, wherever it resides, must be subject to challenge, transparency, and accountability. Numbers may seem neutral. But when they decide the terms of human participation, they become political. And when they define who gets to live fully and who must navigate the world under suspicion, they are no longer just scores. They are sentences.

Normalization and the Numb

The most effective systems of control are not the ones that spark fear—they are the ones that feel normal. When surveillance becomes routine, when restrictions become policy, when indignities become features of daily life, resistance doesn't vanish—it evaporates. Not with force, but with familiarity. What shocks us at first is slowly reclassified as acceptable. The injustice remains; only our sensitivity to it changes. This is how control becomes cultural, not just structural.

The psychology of normalization is subtle but decisive. It doesn't require belief or agreement. It only requires repetition. When a new measure is introduced—mandatory facial scans at airports, location tracking for health compliance, algorithmic content filtering—there may be protest, hesitation, even outrage. But as time passes, the design doesn't change; our threshold does. We adapt. We stop asking questions. We stop noticing. *This is not consent. It's habituation.*

Take facial recognition in public spaces. In many cities, initial deployment met resistance. Civil liberties organisations warned of overreach, data misuse, and racial bias. But the rollouts continued. At first, facial scans were used at airports to "streamline boarding." Then at sports venues, then train stations. Now, they're being trialled in supermarkets. The stated purpose shifts—from security to convenience to personalisation—but the underlying mechanism is constant: real-time biometric monitoring in public life. Once that infrastructure is embedded, even partial removal feels disruptive. What was once invasive now feels merely efficient.

The same pattern can be observed in the normalisation of keyword censorship and automated takedowns on social media platforms. Initially, users were alert to the implications: Who decides what counts as misinformation? What mechanisms are in place for appeal? But those questions faded as the systems remained. Users grew accustomed to the idea that certain posts might be removed, or accounts suspended, often without explanation. Terms of service evolved quietly, moderation expanded, and the culture adjusted. Today, many users engage on platforms with an implicit awareness of the boundaries, rarely voiced but broadly understood. Content is self-filtered not because of explicit pressure, but because people have internalised the limits.

This is not a passive phenomenon. It is actively maintained through language, interface, and institutional messaging. New measures are introduced not as restrictions, but as upgrades—smart borders, intelligent moderation, adaptive authentication. The branding is strategic. By presenting systems of control as improvements, they are reframed as progress. Once framed that way, opposing them is easily dismissed as resistance to innovation, or worse, as recklessness. The debate shifts from whether the system is just to whether it is functioning. And if it's functioning well—if it's fast, sleek, or seamless—questions of power are postponed indefinitely.

The danger here is not just technical or legal. It is emotional. As systems of control become embedded, *we feel less.* What would have once felt like a violation now barely registers. This desensitisation is not apathy—it's exhaustion. People are bombarded with constant prompts for consent, flooded with terms they don't read, tracked by tools they don't understand, and excluded by systems they can't appeal. The human response to such a landscape is often resignation. If everything is monitored, what's the point in resisting? If every device collects data, why care which one does it slightly more invasively?

This resignation creates fertile ground for authoritarian drift—not through dramatic declarations, but through a series of technical adjustments, policy tweaks, and platform decisions that quietly reshape the conditions of civic life. Restrictions on movement become pilot programmes. Data sharing becomes cross-agency integration. Public dissent becomes algorithmic risk. Each step is manageable, explainable, even rational. But the cumulative effect is a society less free, less reflective, and less able to mount meaningful resistance because the architecture of control has been embedded into the infrastructure of daily life.

Consider the shift in airport security protocols after 2001. What began as a response to crisis has become the global norm: removing shoes, discarding liquids, full-body scans. Travellers now expect these rituals, even when their effectiveness is questioned. They are not evaluated for efficacy—they are simply part of the process. Over time, even those most sceptical comply automatically. The same logic applies to digital protocols. When two-factor authentication begins requiring biometric scans tied to national databases, the user may balk at first. But when the process is tied to salary disbursement, medical records, or school access, that hesitation is overridden by necessity. Normalisation follows not from belief but from dependence.

Dependency accelerates desensitisation. The more essential the system, the harder it becomes to question its legitimacy. This is evident in countries where digital ID systems are now mandatory for everything from voting to receiving healthcare. Even citizens who distrust the system comply—because the cost of non-compliance is exclusion. And once the system becomes the gatekeeper, the scope of its power no longer needs to be justified. It simply needs to remain operational.

This is the architecture of numbness: technical systems designed to be invisible, social environments built to discourage friction, and institutional processes that extract participation through fatigue rather than force. People don't stop caring because they are indifferent. They stop caring because the structures around them teach them that caring doesn't matter. Over time, silence becomes adaptive. Submission becomes sensible. And what was once alarming becomes merely the backdrop of modern life.

Resisting this drift requires a shift not in tools, but in awareness. The first act is to *notice what you've stopped noticing.* Which systems do you no longer question? Which compromises feel inevitable? Which updates have changed what you consider "normal"? These are not nostalgic questions. They are diagnostic. They help locate where control has been naturalised. And only by locating it can we begin to evaluate it again—not as something we've accepted, but as something that still requires justification.

Outrage is a limited resource. But vigilance is not. Staying alert to creeping authoritarianism doesn't require dramatic protest. It requires careful attention to how consent is manufactured, how habits are trained, and how expectations are lowered. It means treating every "upgrade" with curiosity. It means refusing to call something "standard" until you understand who made it so, and why. It means remembering that *normal* is not a neutral category. It is a verdict delivered by power.

There is no need to romanticise disruption or glorify resistance. But there is a need—an urgent one—to recover the capacity to feel where power is being quietly exercised. Not just to notice injustice, but to stay sensitive to it. To refuse the comfort of forgetting. And to rebuild, wherever possible, the conditions that allow outrage to remain an appropriate response—not a nostalgic one. Because when numbness becomes the default, authoritarianism no longer needs to announce itself. It just continues. Unchallenged. Unfelt. Unseen.

Chapter 3

The Currency of Compliance

Money has never been just a medium of exchange. It has always been a form of governance—a system of permissions, conditions, and expectations, backed not only by banks but by norms and laws. What is changing now, at an accelerating pace, is the degree to which money itself is becoming programmable, conditional, and algorithmically enforced. The shift from physical to digital currencies is not just a technological transition—it is a political transformation. *We are moving from an economy where money represents freedom to one where it can increasingly dictate behaviour.*

This chapter begins with the recognition that the infrastructure of modern money is no longer neutral. It is engineered. Whether through the rollout of Central Bank Digital Currencies (CBDCs), the disappearance of physical cash, or the proliferation of payment platforms with embedded rules and filters, we are seeing the convergence of financial architecture and behavioural control. Currency is no longer just about what you *can* buy; it is also about what you *should*, *must not*, or *will be incentivised* to buy. This is not hypothetical. It is being tested, implemented, and normalised in real time.

To understand the stakes, we must move beyond debates over inflation, central bank policy, or crypto speculation and look instead at how money is being used as a governance tool. Programmable currency—money that can carry embedded rules, expiry dates, or use-case restrictions—is not merely a digital upgrade. It allows governments and institutions to enforce compliance without passing legislation. Want to stimulate local economies? Programme funds to work only within certain postcodes. Want to curb alcohol consumption? Make welfare disbursements ineligible for use at liquor stores. Want to penalise protest activity? Restrict access to travel, lodging, or payment services for flagged individuals. In each case, the lever is financial. The mechanism is invisible. The effect is decisive.

Consider the emerging architecture of CBDCs. Dozens of central banks—

China's PBOC, the ECB, the Bank of England, and the Federal Reserve, among others—are exploring or piloting digital currencies that sit alongside or eventually replace cash. These systems offer speed, traceability, and centralised oversight. They allow fine-tuned monetary policy at the transactional level: money that can be turned off, redirected, or reconditioned. China's e-CNY already includes pilot features that can limit how funds are used and how long they remain valid. This programmability, while marketed as a tool for efficiency and fraud prevention, introduces a new paradigm: *money as code-bound behaviour management*. It's not just what money can do—it's what it can make you do.

But digital currency isn't the only vector of control. The steady retreat of cash itself is reshaping civil liberties. In India, the 2016 demonetisation initiative—ostensibly aimed at curbing black-market transactions and counterfeit currency—led to sudden and severe liquidity shocks across the informal economy. Street vendors, day labourers, and small traders were disproportionately affected. More importantly, it sent a signal: access to currency could be revoked overnight, and participation in the economy was contingent on state-sanctioned forms of money. Since then, India has aggressively promoted digital payments, often in partnership with private platforms. Convenience has improved—but so has traceability. Every transaction now leaves a data trail. That trail can be used to build profiles, predict behaviour, or enforce compliance.

Sweden offers a different model—one of near-total voluntary transition. Physical cash usage has plummeted to under 10 percent of transactions. Most shops, buses, and public services no longer accept cash. The benefits are clear: reduced robbery, efficient accounting, and a seamless consumer experience. But the cost is less obvious. When cash disappears, so does unmediated exchange. Every payment becomes a form of data entry. Every interaction requires permission from intermediaries. And in emergencies—whether political unrest, technical failure, or cyberattack—resilience is diminished. *Cash is not just currency; it is a fallback. Without it, financial systems become brittle, exclusionary, and vulnerable to abuse.*

The potential for that abuse is not theoretical. It is already visible in the selective application of financial controls to marginalise dissent and enforce ideological conformity. In Canada, during the Freedom Convoy protests in 2022, the federal government invoked emergency powers to freeze bank accounts and suspend insurance policies of protest participants. This action bypassed normal legal processes and was implemented through direct communication with financial institutions. In effect, protestors were de-banked—not through arrest or court order, but through financial incapacitation. No due process. No appeal. The message was clear: *financial infrastructure can and will be weaponised.*

Similar tactics are increasingly common on digital platforms. PayPal has shut down accounts for reasons ranging from alleged misinformation to political activism, often without explanation or recourse. Crowdfunding sites like GoFundMe and Stripe have selectively suspended campaigns deemed controversial or non-compliant with platform policies. These are not minor events. For small organisations or individuals, account freezes can mean the collapse of livelihood. And because these are private companies, traditional protections—such as freedom of speech or access to essential services—do not apply. The terms of service replace the rule of law.

This is monetary redlining—not in the traditional sense of geographic exclusion, but in behavioural and ideological terms. Individuals and groups are being assessed not just by creditworthiness, but by *alignment*. Alignment with norms, with terms, with prevailing narratives. Financial inclusion becomes conditional. You are not entitled to transact—you are *permitted* to, until you are not.

Parallel to these overt controls is a subtler mechanism: *debt*. If programmable money is the carrot and monetary redlining is the stick, debt is the tether. It shapes behaviour not through explicit commands, but through long-term incentives and dependencies. Student loans, for instance, do more than finance education. They shape career choices, mobility, family planning, and even political expression. When repayment obligations stretch over decades, the debtor's autonomy is constrained—not just economically, but psychologically. Certain risks become unaffordable. Certain forms of protest—such as striking or civil disobedience—become too costly.

In the Global South, microfinance programmes have often been promoted as tools for empowerment. But when structured poorly, they reproduce the same dynamics of dependency and control. Borrowers who default risk not only financial penalties but social shaming and exclusion from community services. In some cases, biometric data is tied to microcredit access, linking identity directly to compliance. The borrower is not simply a customer; they are a behavioural subject. Debt becomes not just an economic condition, but a mode of governance.

What unites these phenomena is their subtlety. None of them involve armed enforcement, dramatic decrees, or visible repression. They operate through infrastructure—financial rails, digital wallets, authentication protocols, behavioural scoring systems. The interface is often elegant. The user experience is streamlined. The control is embedded. *This is the currency of compliance: a monetary system that encourages participation by design, disciplines deviation through silence, and reshapes autonomy through invisible nudges.*

This chapter will explore each of these dynamics in detail. It will show how money is no longer simply a store of value, but a programmable script for behaviour. It will examine how the disappearance of cash affects civil liberties and democratic resilience. It will expose the ways in which financial institutions—both public and private—are being used to police ideology and suppress dissent. And it will interrogate the moral architecture of debt: not just who owes what, but what that obligation produces in terms of compliance, conformity, and control.

The question is not whether we should embrace digital payments or reform monetary systems. It is whether we are prepared to treat those systems as political technologies—capable of enabling freedom or enforcing conformity, depending on how they are built, governed, and resisted. We are no longer negotiating with currency as a neutral tool. We are negotiating with systems that have the capacity to encode values, automate consequences, and reshape citizenship itself. This chapter will give readers the tools to see how those negotiations are unfolding—and what is at stake when the medium of exchange becomes a medium of influence.

"Programmable Money, Programmable Behavior":

The digitalisation of money is not merely a change in format—it is a change in function. What was once a static store of value now becomes dynamic, conditional, and governed by code. Central Bank Digital Currencies (CBDCs) are being positioned as the next logical step in monetary innovation, promising faster transactions, reduced fraud, and greater financial inclusion. But behind the sleek user interfaces and policy briefings lies a more profound transformation: *money is being rewritten as a mechanism of behavioural programming.*

To understand the gravity of this shift, it is essential to grasp what distinguishes a CBDC from existing forms of digital payment. Debit cards, mobile wallets, and bank transfers are all digital, but they operate on top of traditional monetary infrastructure. They are intermediated, reversible, and subject to varying degrees of privacy and legal protection. A CBDC, by contrast, is money itself—issued directly by the central bank, programmable at the point of origin, and integrated into a unified national ledger. This is not simply a cash replacement. It is a sovereign system capable of tracking, restricting, and shaping economic behaviour in real time.

China has taken the lead in developing and piloting a CBDC with behavioural functionality. The e-CNY, or digital yuan, has been rolled out in over 20 cities, with millions of residents participating in trials. At a technical level, the system allows authorities to embed rules directly into currency units—expiry dates, geographical restrictions, and transaction limits. This means that a stimulus payment, for example, can be made to vanish if not spent within a certain timeframe, or constrained to use in a designated district. The effect is twofold: economic policy becomes more targeted, and user behaviour becomes more predictable. There is no need to persuade, legislate, or nudge. The currency itself does the work.

Proponents argue that such tools offer extraordinary policy flexibility. Central banks can stimulate demand, curb speculation, prevent hoarding, or encourage consumption with surgical precision. But the implications extend far beyond economics. When money can be restricted based on who you are, where you are, or what you are trying to purchase, it ceases to be neutral. It becomes conditional access. What you spend, where you spend, and even if you're *allowed* to spend, becomes contingent on compliance—not with laws, but with evolving parameters set by designers, bureaucrats, or machine-learning algorithms.

The justification is often public interest: reducing corruption, targeting subsidies, improving welfare delivery. But once such tools exist, their logic can be repurposed. A subsidy that expires in thirty days can evolve into a benefit that is revoked for rule violations. A currency restricted to specific sectors for economic recovery can become a mechanism for moral governance. In authoritarian states, this is explicit. In democratic ones, it is buried in policy detail. The mechanism remains the same: *control embedded at the monetary level.*

Critics of CBDCs are often dismissed as alarmist or ideologically opposed to state intervention. But the concern is not about digitalisation per se—it is about *programmability.* It is one thing to pay with a digital token. It is another when that token comes with rules you didn't choose, can't inspect, and have no right to challenge. This is the difference between a tool and an instrument of rule. When financial infrastructure enforces behaviour through invisible mechanisms, consent becomes irrelevant. You are not being coerced. You are being preconditioned.

Western democracies are moving more cautiously but not without intent. The European Central Bank is exploring a digital euro, with public consultations revealing a strong interest in privacy safeguards. However, the technical specifications under consideration—such as individual wallets managed by licensed intermediaries and transaction-level controls—suggest a potential for surveillance and restriction, even if undeclared at launch. The Bank of England has similarly stated that its CBDC design would avoid programmability "by the central bank" but could support functionality through private-sector wallets. This is a sleight of hand. The programmability doesn't disappear—it is simply outsourced.

The argument often made is that existing payment systems already permit such control. Banks freeze accounts, credit card companies block transactions, and apps like Venmo or PayPal enforce terms of service. But these are fragmented, contestable, and jurisdiction-bound. A CBDC, by contrast, is a monolithic structure. It centralises monetary function, strips away intermediaries, and codifies behavioural logic into the architecture itself. *What law once enforced overtly, design can now enforce silently.*

Moreover, programmability is not limited to state-directed controls. Commercial entities can be authorised to build layers atop CBDC infrastructure—loyalty schemes, incentive mechanisms, real-time scoring. This creates a feedback loop where behaviour is not only tracked but shaped in return. Consumers receive discounts for "good" choices, face friction for "bad" ones, and gradually internalise a logic of compliance-as-convenience. The currency becomes a training tool. The user becomes a data point.

Consider a hypothetical future where climate goals are tied to personal carbon budgets. The CBDC could be integrated with purchase history to monitor emissions. Exceed your quota for the month? Your funds may still exist—but they're temporarily ineligible for use on petrol or flights. This may sound futuristic, but several governments and corporations are already experimenting with similar scoring systems, including Mastercard's partnership with fintech companies to offer carbon tracking per transaction. *The infrastructure for behaviour-linked currency is not in development—it's in deployment.*

Yet the challenge is not only technical or political—it is conceptual. Most people still think of money as fungible and universal. A dollar is a dollar. A pound is a pound. This assumption masks the deeper shift underway. Programmable currency is *contextual money*: its value and utility depend not on what you have, but on what the system permits you to do with it. This breaks the core idea of economic agency. Your money is no longer *yours* in the functional sense. It is *yours conditionally.*

There are also second-order effects that deserve scrutiny. The programmability of money can lead to the automation of sanctions, the scaling of economic discrimination, and the erosion of informal economies that rely on cash. In fragile states or regions with limited digital infrastructure, a premature shift to programmable money could deepen inequality and financial exclusion. More subtly, it could normalise surveillance, not by mandate but by default. People stop questioning monitoring when it's baked into daily function. They stop resisting when control feels frictionless.

But the issue is not just what governments *might* do with programmable currency. It's what they'll no longer need to do through legislation, courts, or persuasion. If spending can be directed, limited, or reversed without public process, then the relationship between citizen and state is radically altered. The judiciary is sidestepped. The ballot box becomes less relevant. Political dissent need not be criminalised—it can simply be rendered economically unviable.

This transformation does not require total adoption to be effective. As programmable currencies become available, those who opt out will face increasing difficulty participating in formal commerce. As private services migrate to CBDC-compatible systems, cash users and critics will find themselves excluded by design. The drift toward compliance will be enforced not by law but by limitation. And unlike traditional monetary policy, there is no public debate about where that line should be drawn. It is technical, procedural, and operational—shielded from scrutiny by its very complexity.

To be clear, not all programmability is malign. There are legitimate uses—automated tax remittance, fraud prevention, conditional grants—that can improve transparency and efficiency. But these features must be designed with explicit boundaries, democratic oversight, and fail-safes. A currency is not just a payment method. It is a social contract. When its rules change silently, that contract is rewritten without consent.

This is the central issue at stake in the global transition to programmable money. The design choices being made today—often in technocratic circles, policy papers, or software protocols—will determine the boundaries of economic freedom for decades to come. The framing matters. Are we building digital tools to enhance autonomy, or to choreograph compliance? Are we giving people more agency, or merely more options within increasingly narrow lanes?

What makes programmable currency so effective as a control mechanism is its invisibility. There are no flashing warnings, no threats of punishment. Just terms and conditions that shift beneath your feet. Just permissions granted—or denied—by code. The user doesn't rebel. The user adapts. And in that adaptation, something profound is lost: the idea that value, once earned, is yours to decide how to use.

This chapter begins here—not with monetary theory, but with the anatomy of silent constraint. The pages that follow will examine how CBDCs are being implemented, what behavioural assumptions they encode, and how their programmability reconfigures the balance between trust, autonomy, and authority. We are not debating the future of currency. We are confronting its present—and what it is being engineered to become.

"The Vanishing Cash Frontier":

There was a time—not long ago—when the ability to hand over a banknote in exchange for goods or services was so mundane as to be unremarkable. Today, the absence of that option is no longer a technological novelty. It is fast becoming a policy goal. Governments, financial institutions, and technology providers across the globe are converging on a shared ambition: a cashless society. This transition is often framed as progress—efficient, secure, modern. But behind the glossy packaging lies a more consequential story: *the quiet erosion of civil liberties through the disappearance of physical money.*

Cash is more than a payment tool. It is a form of privacy, autonomy, and democratic access. It allows for anonymous exchange, protects against surveillance, and enables participation without approval from a platform, a provider, or the state. It does not require a smartphone, a stable internet connection, or a verifiable identity. Its value is inherent and its use is offline. In a world increasingly shaped by digital controls, cash functions as a form of sovereignty—for the individual, and for communities that exist outside the reach of digital finance.

India offers one of the most dramatic case studies of how cash can be eliminated—not gradually, but by decree. In November 2016, Prime Minister Narendra Modi announced that the two highest denomination notes, which made up over 85 percent of the currency in circulation, would be invalid overnight. Officially, the objective was to combat black money, counterfeit currency, and corruption. In practice, the policy caused widespread economic disruption, disproportionately affecting rural populations, informal workers, and small-scale traders. For many, cash was not a choice—it was the only viable means of exchange. ATMs ran dry. Queues stretched for hours. Daily wage earners lost income. And yet, despite the upheaval, the state declared the move a success and doubled down on its digital agenda.

What followed was a push to replace physical transactions with biometric-based payments. The Aadhaar identity system, linked to mobile numbers and bank accounts, became the cornerstone of the new digital financial ecosystem. Citizens were encouraged—sometimes coerced—into adopting digital wallets, QR code payments, and unified payment interfaces (UPI). The narrative was inclusion, but the reality was enforcement. Subsidies and welfare payments were routed through linked accounts. Cash withdrawals were restricted in some regions. The message was clear: adapt to the digital framework or risk being left behind.

Sweden, by contrast, arrived at a cashless economy through a different route—voluntary adoption led by commercial innovation. Over the past decade, cash usage has plummeted. As of 2022, less than 10 percent of consumer transactions involved cash. Many businesses no longer accept it. Public transport systems have gone digital-only. Even churches take donations via card or app. The shift is often celebrated as a model of efficiency and trust in institutions. But even in Sweden, cracks have emerged. The elderly, people with disabilities, and residents in rural areas have raised concerns about exclusion. The country's central bank has warned that the decline of cash poses risks to resilience and democratic control over the payment system. In response, legislation has been proposed to ensure that banks continue to provide access to cash services. But this is a rear-guard action against a cultural tide that has already turned.

Australia offers yet another angle—where policy, pandemic, and market forces accelerated the decline of cash. Even before COVID-19, Australia was rapidly adopting contactless payments. The pandemic acted as a catalyst. Fears of viral transmission led businesses to refuse physical currency. Government stimulus packages were delivered through digital channels. And mobile banking apps surged in popularity. By 2023, ATM usage had declined by more than 50 percent from its peak. The infrastructure to support cash—branches, machines, even coin-handling services—has been quietly dismantled. Yet few public debates have been held about the long-term implications.

The move towards a cashless society is not simply a technological inevitability. It is a series of policy and commercial choices that, taken together, *narrow the range of economic autonomy available to citizens.* Without cash, every transaction becomes trackable. Every purchase feeds into a data profile. The power to participate economically is mediated by credentials, platforms, and algorithms. A frozen account, a denied transaction, or a technical glitch becomes not a nuisance, but a total lockout.

Moreover, the centralisation of financial data introduces systemic vulnerabilities. In a cashless world, outages, cyberattacks, or policy missteps can paralyse entire economies. In 2021, a major Australian bank experienced a digital payments outage that left customers unable to make purchases for hours. No cash, no backup. Just waiting for the system to reboot. What was once a private contingency—a few banknotes tucked away for emergencies—is now a political question about the design of national infrastructure.

Cash also plays a critical role in safeguarding dissent and diversity. Activists, informal workers, and marginalised communities often rely on cash to operate without surveillance or gatekeeping. When protests erupt, when regimes change, when systems fail, cash remains a tool of resilience. It does not discriminate, and it does not record. It is not perfect, but it is permissionless. In contrast, digital systems can be weaponised. Transactions can be flagged, accounts frozen, or histories used as evidence. The act of buying a book, donating to a cause, or travelling to a location becomes a matter of record—potentially scrutinised, retroactively judged, or penalised.

This is not a theoretical concern. During Canada's 2022 Freedom Convoy protests, authorities froze bank accounts of individuals associated with the movement, relying on emergency powers. Payment platforms were asked to report and restrict activity. This was not a court order or a conviction. It was financial policing—swift, sweeping, and algorithmically enforced. In such a system, neutrality disappears. Finance becomes a tool of governance.

Supporters of digital payments argue that cash enables crime, tax evasion, and shadow economies. These concerns are not without merit. But they are often overstated and selectively applied. The overwhelming majority of cash use is legal and mundane. Moreover, digital systems are not immune to abuse—they simply concentrate risk in fewer hands. Fraud, hacking, and surveillance are not eliminated; they are reshaped. The solution is not to abolish cash, but to improve regulatory mechanisms across both domains.

There is also an equity dimension. A cashless world assumes equal access to digital tools, literacy, and infrastructure. In practice, this is rarely the case.

In India, connectivity remains uneven. In parts of rural Australia, digital exclusion is real. Elderly populations, people with disabilities, and those facing economic hardship often lack the means or confidence to navigate app-based banking. The design of digital-first systems frequently neglects these realities, framing non-adoption as resistance rather than exclusion.

A democracy that values choice must preserve multiple pathways to participation. Digital payments should be an option, not a mandate. Cash should not be treated as an obsolete relic, but as a civic instrument—low-tech, high-trust, and widely accessible. Its disappearance is not merely a question of efficiency. It is a bellwether of how much autonomy we are willing to cede for convenience.

The vanishing of cash is not just about coins and notes. It is about the disappearance of friction in systems of control. When every transaction flows through digital rails, the capacity for intervention expands exponentially. Spend patterns can be analysed. Risk profiles can be generated. Permissions can be revoked. The boundaries of acceptable behaviour can be defined—and enforced—not by law, but by code.

This is not a call for regression. It is a demand for reckoning. What are we sacrificing when we remove the last offline option from the economy? What values are embedded in the platforms that now mediate our spending? Who gets to decide the terms of participation, and who bears the cost of exclusion?

These questions must be answered before cash becomes a memory. Because once the infrastructure is gone, it will not be easily rebuilt. And by then, the choice may no longer be ours to make.

"Monetary Redlining":

Financial systems were once understood as neutral architecture—tools for commerce, not conduct. But that understanding has become dangerously outdated. Today, money is not merely a medium of exchange; it is increasingly a mechanism of discipline. The line between financial access and political compliance has begun to blur. *Monetary redlining*—the selective restriction of financial services based on ideology, behaviour, or association—has become an emerging form of control, difficult to detect yet profoundly consequential. Unlike the overt censorship of speech or protest, monetary restrictions often escape public scrutiny. They are bureaucratic, opaque, and enforced through private intermediaries rather than courts or legislatures.

The language of terms and conditions replaces the rule of law. A click on a digital dashboard replaces due process. And a transaction denied carries no explanation beyond "policy violation." When financial tools become instruments of enforcement, entire populations can be shaped—not by debate or law, but by silent, systemic design.

Consider the case of PayPal, one of the largest global payment platforms. Over the past decade, it has banned or suspended accounts belonging to individuals, organisations, and publications on grounds ranging from "hate speech" to "misinformation" to "violation of use policies." Some cases have involved clearly harmful actors. Others have been murkier—journalists, whistleblowers, independent media, or political commentators whose content falls outside the mainstream but does not violate any law. The decisions are often unilateral, without transparency or appeal. Funds can be frozen. Donations can be withheld. An entire revenue stream can vanish with an automated email. This is not a courtroom; it is a customer service portal with no obligation to explain.

The architecture of these systems means that enforcement can happen at scale, without accountability. A payment processor's algorithms may flag certain phrases, topics, or donation patterns as risky. A backend risk management team may respond not with evidence, but with pre-emptive closure. There is no need to prove intent. No chance to contest the charge. The reputational damage is immediate; the financial impact is real. And the message is unmistakable: toe the line, or be unbanked.

The political dimensions of this approach came sharply into view during Canada's 2022 Freedom Convoy protests. In response to widespread demonstrations against COVID-19 mandates, the Canadian government invoked emergency powers to freeze the bank accounts of participants and supporters. These were not individuals convicted of crimes. Many were simply donors whose names appeared in leaked crowdfunding lists. The rationale was public safety. But the method was financial immobilisation. Banks and fintech companies were asked to freeze assets without court orders. Insurance policies were suspended. Credit cards were flagged. This marked a turning point: the use of financial infrastructure to punish civil disobedience—*not by passing new laws, but by activating existing networks of compliance.*

The implications are far-reaching. In traditional governance models, punishment follows adjudication. An independent judiciary reviews evidence, interprets the law, and delivers judgement. But in the emerging model of financial enforcement, platforms act as both judge and jailer. Their rules are elastic. Their actions are extralegal. And their reach is growing. What began as moderation of commerce—limiting fraud, stopping money laundering—has expanded into moderation of ideology.

This shift is not limited to Western democracies. In China, the use of financial sanctions to enforce conformity is explicit and institutionalised. The Social Credit System, though still fragmented in its implementation, incorporates financial penalties into behavioural scoring. A low score can restrict access to loans, employment, travel, or even schooling. Individuals who criticise the government, default on debts, or engage in "untrustworthy" conduct can find themselves locked out of everyday functions. Cashless payments—ubiquitous through platforms like WeChat Pay and Alipay—make enforcement seamless. A user flagged by the system may find their digital wallet disabled, or their ability to buy tickets denied. *There is no arrest, no trial—only a QR code that stops working.*

What makes monetary redlining distinct is its subtleness. Unlike censorship, which draws attention, or incarceration, which prompts resistance, financial exclusion often masquerades as technical error, policy update, or private decision-making. There is no banner warning the public. No protest visible on the street. The punished individual is simply excluded—unable to rent, transact, or operate, often without knowing who made the decision or why.

This lack of visibility creates a dangerous asymmetry. Power is centralised, but responsibility is diffused. A bank may blame the regulator. A fintech firm may cite internal policy. A government may deny involvement. The user is left with no redress, no clarity, and no tools to fight back. Worse, as financial ecosystems become more consolidated, alternative pathways vanish. If one bank denies you, you switch to another. But if every payment processor follows similar protocols, the exit doors shrink. A few keystrokes can make someone economically nonviable.

Economic sanctions—traditionally deployed as foreign policy tools—illustrate this logic on a global scale. The United States and European Union have used sanctions to isolate regimes, punish violations of international norms, and exert pressure without military force. But sanctions do not only target governments. Increasingly, they affect banks, businesses, and individuals—sometimes based on loosely defined affiliations. Entire populations can suffer collateral damage. Civilians may lose access to medicines, students may be unable to pay tuition abroad, or citizens may have savings frozen in foreign accounts.

These actions are not always unjustified. Sanctions can be strategic tools. But their expansion into the digital financial layer introduces new risks. Cryptocurrency exchanges, crowdfunding platforms, and digital banks are now being drawn into the sanctioning apparatus. Compliance becomes a design feature—pre-emptive, algorithmic, and absolute. The assumption is that control must be total to be effective. But such control carries a cost: *the erosion of financial pluralism and democratic resilience.*

There is also the problem of ideological drift. Once financial exclusion becomes an accepted tool, its definition tends to expand. Today's targets may be extremists or criminals. Tomorrow's may be dissidents, critics, or outliers. The line is not fixed; it is redrawn with each crisis, campaign, or scandal. Over time, the criteria for redlining can shift from security to conformity—an ever-tightening circle of acceptable behaviour determined by those who design the rails.

We are not facing a sudden collapse of rights, but a slow reconfiguration of infrastructure. Financial systems—once passive channels—are becoming active governors. The question is no longer whether you can access money, but whether you can access it *without being profiled, scored, or judged.* Can you remain financially viable without ideological compliance? Can you dissent without losing your livelihood?

The answers will depend on how these systems evolve. There is room for reform. Greater transparency in payment platform decisions. Legal frameworks that define due process for account closures. Mandates for financial neutrality in essential services. But such measures require political will—and public awareness. Most importantly, they require us to recognise financial access not merely as a privilege, but as a civil right in the digital age.

Because when money itself becomes conditional—on your politics, your speech, your associations—freedom is no longer a constitutional guarantee. It is a product, subject to cancellation. The account may still exist. But the user, effectively, does not.

"Debt as a Design Tool":

Debt is rarely presented as an instrument of governance. It is framed instead as a transaction—a loan, an agreement, a financial lifeline. But behind the contracts and interest rates lies something far more structural: *a system of behavioural engineering, carefully calibrated to guide, constrain, and extract.* Debt does not merely bind individuals financially; it organises time, priorities, and decision-making. The terms dictate more than repayment—they shape life trajectories. In modern economies, debt has quietly evolved into a regulatory tool more pervasive than law, more intimate than policy, and more coercive than it appears.

The most visible arena where this dynamic plays out is higher education. Student debt in the United States exceeds $1.7 trillion, burdening over 40 million individuals. This is not simply a financial issue—it is a system of behavioural design. A young adult, typically without assets or financial literacy, is presented with a binary choice: take on debt, or forfeit access to the professional economy. The structure is not framed as coercion, but as opportunity. Yet once enrolled, debt begins to organise behaviour. Graduates postpone marriage, delay home ownership, avoid riskier careers, and often seek stability over exploration. Debt does not merely demand repayment; *it silently narrows the imagination of the future.*

The repayment structure also locks individuals into long-term compliance. For many, default is not just a financial penalty—it carries consequences for credit scores, employment eligibility, housing access, and even professional licensing in some U.S. states. What began as a private loan becomes a public constraint. The borrower is not simply paying down a balance—they are performing reliability, signalling discipline, and avoiding administrative punishment. This behavioural script is often invisible to those outside the system, but deeply familiar to those within it.

Student loans are just one expression. The same design logic is evident in microcredit schemes in developing economies. Once hailed as a revolution in economic empowerment, microfinance has since revealed a darker side: *the individualisation of poverty and the moralisation of debt.* In countries like Bangladesh and India, group lending structures require participants to guarantee each other's loans. In theory, this promotes community solidarity. In practice, it creates surveillance and social pressure. Missed payments are not merely financial failings—they become breaches of trust, inviting public shame or exclusion. The message is clear: to be poor is acceptable, but to be unreliable is not.

These schemes often impose interest rates that would be intolerable in formal banking. The justification is risk, but the result is entrapment. Borrowers are steered into cycles of repayment, refinance, and dependency, often using one loan to service another. Debt becomes a permanent condition, not a transitional phase. And critically, it reframes systemic inequality as personal mismanagement. Structural unemployment, healthcare costs, or agricultural failure are not seen as policy issues, but as individual burdens to be carried—and repaid.

Digital finance has amplified these patterns. Fintech platforms now extend credit based not on traditional banking history, but on behavioural data—social media usage, mobile phone activity, or online shopping habits. In Kenya, for example, mobile lenders use real-time data to assess creditworthiness. This enables rapid access to loans—but also introduces a new layer of scrutiny. A person's browsing history or contact list can determine eligibility. *The self becomes collateral.* And once in the system, borrowers are tracked through apps, nudged through push notifications, and penalised through algorithmic scoring.

Such systems are sold as efficiency. In reality, they introduce a form of ambient control—one where debt is no longer about capital, but compliance. Repayment reminders mimic motivational language. Gamified interfaces reward promptness with badges or improved limits. Borrowers are managed not by bank managers, but by UX designers and behavioural economists. This is not accidental. It is intentional design, where the emotional choreography of repayment—guilt, pride, anxiety, satisfaction—is engineered into the product.

A similar shift is visible in housing. In many Western cities, mortgage debt is the price of stability. Owning a home often requires three decades of repayment—a timeline that imposes predictability and anchors lifestyle choices. Mortgage holders are less likely to protest, relocate, or change professions. The debt stabilises neighbourhoods and workforce patterns, but it also disciplines conduct. Homeowners become stakeholders in the status quo—not necessarily by conviction, but by necessity. *Revolt is harder when your credit score is tied to your postcode.*

Even national economies are subject to debt conditioning. International institutions like the IMF and World Bank have long used debt as leverage for policy compliance. Structural adjustment programmes impose reforms—privatisation, austerity, deregulation—as conditions for financing. These are not merely economic suggestions. They are mandates, enforced through contractual obligation. Countries do not vote on them. Citizens do not elect them. The rules are embedded in loan agreements, enforced by disbursement schedules, and monitored by auditors. The result is sovereignty that feels intact, but operates under conditionality.

This model scales down, too. Local governments take on bonds that require balanced budgets. Schools adopt performance metrics tied to funding. Public agencies reorient toward service delivery targets designed by creditors. Debt's power lies not in its size, but in its architecture—it binds future action to past obligation. It turns the promise of growth into a logic of constraint.

What emerges from these examples is a broader insight: *debt functions as a behavioural infrastructure*. It is not imposed through violence, but embedded through norms. It does not require policing; it invites self-regulation. It shifts accountability away from system designers and toward individual actors. The moral vocabulary shifts with it. Borrowers are not subjects of policy—they are consumers of opportunity. If they fail, the narrative is personal. If they succeed, the credit is financial literacy, not systemic design.

This framing obscures structural inequalities. Predatory lending practices, discriminatory interest rates, or exploitative loan terms are reframed as bad choices rather than systemic failures. Worse, this framing enters the cultural psyche. Debt becomes a rite of passage. A test of character. A metric of maturity. Even language adapts: "good debt," "bad debt," "creditworthiness." Each term carries moral weight. Each repayment is not just an economic act, but a performance of virtue.

Yet in accepting this logic, we risk losing sight of its consequences. When debt becomes normalised, freedom is redefined. Freedom no longer means independence from obligation. It means the ability to manage obligations well. A "free" citizen is one who services debt on time, maintains a credit profile, and avoids disruption. This is not freedom as autonomy. It is freedom as solvency.

The design of debt, then, is not merely a financial matter—it is a societal blueprint. It determines who has access, who is trusted, who is mobile, and who is heard. It shapes what people can risk, what they must prioritise, and what they are allowed to imagine. This is why debt must be studied not only as an economic instrument, but as a political technology. It is a system that does not merely reflect inequality—it produces it.

Any serious conversation about liberty, fairness, or agency must reckon with how debt operates—not in theory, but in practice. Who defines the terms. Who sets the rates. Who holds the power to forgive or punish. Because until we confront these structures, debt will continue to do quietly what no law dares to do openly: train obedience, disguise control, and tether the future to the past.

Chapter 4

Data Colonialism in a Post-Land World

Colonialism was never merely about land. It was always about control—of movement, of labour, of classification, of value. Borders were drawn not just on maps, but on bodies. The colonies were laboratories of domination, and empire refined its tools through the granular management of populations: censuses, registries, railroads, plantations. In the post-colonial, post-industrial, post-land world, this control has not disappeared. It has been digitised. And today, *data is the territory being claimed.*

In this emerging empire, the extractive logic of colonialism has found new coordinates. Where natural resources once justified the seizure of territory, now behavioural data serves the same purpose—sourced from the everyday movements, habits, communications, and biometrics of individuals who never agreed to be mined. Their lives become signals. Their identities become variables. Their agency becomes metadata. Extraction no longer requires armies or annexations. It requires apps, sensors, broadband networks, and the language of "innovation." And while the geography has changed, the dynamics remain hauntingly familiar: asymmetry of power, lack of consent, infrastructural imposition, and the unaccountable fusion of public and private interests.

This chapter invites the reader to examine how global tech companies, in partnership with states and financial institutions, are redrawing the frontier of control—not through visible occupation, but through *invisible instrumentation.* The idea of a "digital landgrab" is not metaphorical. It is literal. Countries in the Global South, particularly in Africa and Latin America, are becoming the new territories of surveillance, experimentation, and enforced dependency. Their populations are enrolled into biometric ID programmes, smart city projects, and data-for-aid schemes under the promise of development. In truth, these initiatives often operate as trojan horses for data extraction. The currency is not just economic capital—it is informational sovereignty.

Consider Kenya's Huduma Namba or Ghana's National Digital Property Addressing System. On the surface, these are civic modernisation efforts aimed at inclusion, efficiency, and access. But beneath the surface lies a deeper political economy: Western-backed tech firms and consultants drafting the architecture, foreign cloud servers storing the identities of millions, and opaque policy frameworks governing usage. Citizens are mapped, indexed, and sorted before they fully understand what data they are surrendering or to whom. *Consent becomes a checkbox in a system already designed to function without it.*

Brazil offers another lens. Its smart city initiatives, particularly in São Paulo and Rio de Janeiro, have led to expanded surveillance infrastructures, often justified by urban planning or public safety goals. Yet the result is increased targeting of marginalised communities—particularly Afro-Brazilian and low-income populations—through predictive policing and algorithmic monitoring. These systems claim neutrality, but operationalise historic bias. The city becomes a sensor-rich zone of control where visibility is not a protection but a risk. Those who are most tracked are rarely the ones whose voices shape the policies.

This techno-colonial expansion is not conducted by states alone. It is often the joint venture of Big Tech, development banks, intelligence agencies, and authoritarian regimes bound by strategic mutualism. In exchange for infrastructure, access, or funding, governments hand over citizen data—sometimes knowingly, sometimes by design. Surveillance is recast as a form of modernisation, not suppression. Biometric systems are sold as tools for inclusion, not social stratification. Predictive analytics are marketed as security, not suspicion. The vocabulary of empowerment obscures the machinery of capture.

The United States, through its intelligence-industrial complex, plays a central but often obscured role. Surveillance partnerships brokered between Silicon Valley firms and repressive governments are rarely advertised, but they are functional. Israeli and American companies provide biometric tools to Indian authorities. European firms collaborate with North African border agencies to profile migrants. Chinese platforms export surveillance kits under the banner of "smart governance." The pattern is consistent: regimes gain operational capability, while foreign partners gain access to vast, unregulated data streams.

At the heart of this process is the reduction of identity to database—a phenomenon this chapter names as *the return of the numbered body.* Historically, colonial administrations tracked subjects through passbooks, tribal registries, and caste codes. Today, those same bodies are being logged into systems with more precision and less resistance. Nigeria's National Identification Number (NIN) programme requires citizens to link their ID to phone numbers, bank accounts, and SIM cards. Those who do not comply face deactivation or exclusion from essential services. This is not identification for empowerment. It is identification for discipline.

Contrast this with Estonia's e-ID system—a digital infrastructure often held up as the gold standard of governance. Citizens enjoy streamlined access to services, strong privacy protections, and transparent control over their own data. Yet even in such cases, *participation is still designed on institutional terms*. Opting out is rarely a viable alternative. The model may be more equitable, but the underlying truth remains: when identity becomes infrastructure, the self becomes subordinated to systems. One's legitimacy in society is conditional on visibility and compliance.

A post-land world is not a world without colonisation. It is a world where colonisation takes subtler, more technical forms. Instead of plantations, we have platforms. Instead of chartered companies, we have start-ups backed by venture capital and sanctioned by development ministries. Instead of armies, we have algorithms. And the frontier is no longer a line on a map—it is a layer of metadata over human life.

The challenge, then, is not simply to call out injustice, but to *decode the mechanisms* by which it operates. Data colonialism does not announce itself as conquest. It arrives in the language of progress. It is implemented through dashboards and APIs, not flags and rifles. It functions through logistical mastery, legal ambiguity, and cultural inertia. The systems are not always malevolent—but they are rarely neutral.

This chapter demands that we rethink sovereignty—not as control over territory, but as *control over information flows*. Who governs the databases? Who writes the code? Who profits from compliance? And most critically, who has the right to refuse? Because refusal is what defines true agency. And today, the infrastructures being deployed across the Global South are built precisely to make refusal difficult, if not impossible.

There is nothing inherently wrong with digital infrastructure. Identity systems can protect rights. Smart cities can improve lives. Surveillance, when governed properly, can prevent harm. But that is not what is happening. What is happening is *an asymmetrical restructuring of power*, one interface at a time. This chapter is not about imagining dystopia—it is about interrogating the systems that already shape reality for billions. The aim is not to moralise, but to demystify. To reveal how, when data becomes currency, those without it—or those most exposed by it—become subjects once again.

What follows is an examination of how digital tools, when unchecked, replicate the dynamics of extraction, control, and dispossession. It is an invitation to see past the narratives of inclusion and innovation, and instead ask harder questions about *who is being counted, who is being tracked, and who is doing the counting.* Only by asking these questions can we begin to imagine a future where technology serves people—not power.

The New Extractive Empire

Colonialism has always adapted to its tools. Where European empires once extracted ivory, rubber, and gold, today's powers extract something less tangible but no less valuable: behavioural data. What was once done through gunboats and trading charters is now accomplished with fibre optic cables, app installations, and biometric enrollment campaigns. The theatre of control has shifted, but its logic remains intact. The Global South is again a frontier—not of unclaimed territory, but of *unclaimed informational capital.* The resource now sought is not what lies under the ground, but what flows through people's phones, search histories, facial expressions, and consumption habits. And it is being captured with a precision that old colonisers could only have imagined.

The actors have changed, but the hierarchy is familiar. In this new extractive empire, Big Tech firms sit at the centre. Google, Amazon, Meta, and Microsoft do not carry flags or command navies, but they do dictate the terms of technological dependency. Their infrastructure—cloud services, operating systems, digital platforms—has become foundational to the governance, communication, and economic flows of entire nations. States, particularly those with limited regulatory capacity or urgent development goals, find themselves tethered to foreign technologies that claim to offer modernisation, but often deliver surveillance, capture, and loss of sovereign control.

One of the most significant enablers of this dynamic is the packaging of development aid with digital infrastructure. Foreign governments and multilateral institutions increasingly promote "digital public goods" as essential for economic inclusion and institutional reform. Yet in practice, these projects often come bundled with data pipelines that disproportionately benefit the provider, not the recipient. For example, the World Bank's Identity for Development (ID4D) initiative, which supports the rollout of digital ID systems in low-income countries, has been championed as a way to expand access to services and unlock economic participation. But when implemented without strong privacy laws, transparent governance, or citizen consent, these systems risk becoming surveillance tools in the hands of both local elites and foreign contractors.

India's Aadhaar system is frequently cited as a global model for digital ID infrastructure. What is less discussed is how India's experience has become a prototype for data governance frameworks exported to Africa and Southeast Asia. The architects of Aadhaar—many of whom now work with international agencies or private foundations—have positioned themselves as technical advisors to countries seeking similar reforms. This diffusion of infrastructure design, often under the auspices of "South-South collaboration," masks the asymmetric relationships embedded within. The Aadhaar model centralises biometric data, links identity to welfare access, and creates a unified digital persona across state services. When adopted without adequate legal safeguards, this architecture allows for mass profiling, real-time tracking, and the erosion of anonymity as a civic right.

Consider Nigeria's partnership with Mastercard and other foreign entities to build its National Identity Management Commission (NIMC) framework. The promise was inclusion: better access to banking, health, and government services. But in practice, registration became a prerequisite for mobile phone ownership and even voting. The biometric data collected—fingerprints, facial scans, and demographic details—was stored in systems maintained by a patchwork of public and private operators. Nigerians found themselves required to be visible to the state in exchange for basic entitlements. Yet few understood who had access to this information or how it might be used.

At the heart of this process is a simple dynamic: *data is being extracted faster than rights are being built.* Countries are told they must digitise to develop. But they are rarely given the resources to govern their digitisation on their own terms. They are encouraged to adopt turnkey solutions—cloud platforms, facial recognition software, fintech stacks—that come pre-packaged with embedded terms of use and opaque ownership models. These tools are not neutral. They are political artefacts, built with assumptions about governance, markets, and human behaviour that reflect the values of the entities designing them. And yet, they are being deployed in contexts where accountability mechanisms are still nascent or fragile.

This is not simply a story of exploitation. It is a story of substitution—where sovereignty is traded for speed, and governance is outsourced in the name of efficiency. Rwanda's embrace of Smart Africa initiatives, backed by Chinese and American investors alike, is often lauded as an example of digital progress. Yet much of the country's surveillance capacity is powered by Huawei-built infrastructure, operated in coordination with state security forces. Cameras line the streets of Kigali. Facial recognition is integrated into policing. Citizens are asked to trust that these tools serve public order, not political control. But as with many other countries in the region, there is little independent oversight to verify that this is the case.

Meanwhile, Western firms enjoy the luxury of plausible deniability. Amazon Web Services hosts sensitive government data in regions with weak data protection regimes. Palantir and similar analytics companies sell intelligence platforms to countries with troubling human rights records. Facebook's Free Basics programme, now banned in India, was initially rolled out as a philanthropic initiative offering "free internet" to the poor. What it actually offered was a walled garden—limited access to a handful of curated services that conveniently excluded competitors and gathered extensive behavioural metadata. In practice, it was a form of digital enclosure.

And then there is China. Through its Belt and Road Initiative (BRI) and Digital Silk Road, China has become a leading exporter of surveillance technologies, AI-driven governance tools, and social scoring systems. From Zimbabwe to Ecuador, Chinese firms provide the equipment and training needed to build high-resolution citizen monitoring systems. These are framed as technical partnerships, not political alignments. But the consequences are deeply political. The recipient governments gain tools of control. The provider gains privileged access to national data streams and policy influence.

What distinguishes the new extractive empire from previous forms of colonialism is not just its subtlety, but its speed. Colonial powers of the 19th century spent decades building railroads, telegraphs, and customs systems. Today, a data infrastructure can be implemented in months—if not weeks—using cloud platforms, mobile apps, and biometric devices. Once deployed, these systems are hard to undo. They generate lock-in effects: technical dependencies, legal frameworks, bureaucratic routines. The population adapts to the infrastructure faster than regulators can respond to its risks. By the time questions are raised about consent, ownership, or control, the architecture is already embedded.

This is why the language of "data is the new oil" is both misleading and revealing. It is misleading because, unlike oil, data is not finite. It can be collected continuously and in greater volume. But it is revealing because, like oil, data requires extraction, processing, and infrastructure to be turned into value. And as with the history of resource extraction, the profits flow to those who control the pipelines, not those who generate the raw material. In this case, the pipelines are fibre networks, cloud servers, and proprietary algorithms. The raw material is you.

This article does not argue against digital infrastructure or international cooperation. Development requires both. But it *does* argue for a clearer understanding of power asymmetries. When development aid is conditioned on technology adoption, when national data is stored on foreign servers, when citizens must comply with biometric mandates to access welfare, *we must ask who is developing whom.* Sovereignty is not just about borders anymore—it is about control over one's informational ecosystem. And too often, that control is quietly slipping away.

The new extractive empire is not violent in the conventional sense. But it is deeply coercive. It captures populations through design rather than force, through code rather than law, through partnerships rather than occupation. Its legitimacy is bolstered by the language of progress, its mechanisms are hidden behind technical complexity, and its effects are normalised through infrastructure. By the time it becomes visible, it is often too late.

Understanding this empire requires more than technical literacy. It requires *political imagination.* We must think critically about who sets the terms of digital transformation, who builds the tools of identity and access, and who benefits from the data that flows through every interaction, transaction, and registration. The story of the 21st century will not be one of land disputes. It will be one of data disputes. And the battleground is already here.

Digital Landgrabs

When land was the most valuable asset on earth, colonial powers surveyed, partitioned, and claimed it with boundary stones, treaties, and force. Today, the battleground has shifted, but the logic remains. In a world where data is capital, entire populations are now being mapped, tagged, and profiled—not for ownership of territory, but for control of informational terrain. These new frontiers are not forests or rivers, but sensor grids, data lakes, and behavioural profiles. And the conquest doesn't come through invasion. It arrives through infrastructure.

Digital landgrabs operate on the premise that connectivity equals progress. The language is modernisation, urban development, smart governance. But the reality is often mass data capture, executed through opaque partnerships between states and corporations, without meaningful public understanding or consent. Beneath the allure of smart cities lies a deeper transformation: the population becomes legible not just to itself, but to an external gaze—one that turns daily life into analysable flows of traceable behaviour.

Kenya's Konza Technopolis is among the most emblematic examples of this dynamic. Framed as "Africa's Silicon Savannah," Konza was marketed as a leapfrog opportunity: a purpose-built smart city promising innovation hubs, data centres, and tech-driven education. What's less discussed is how its development strategy hinged on the integration of biometric IDs, surveillance infrastructure, and pervasive data collection mechanisms. The National Integrated Identity Management System (NIIMS), known locally as Huduma Namba, was positioned as the linchpin of national digital transformation. But critics quickly observed that it bore all the hallmarks of a data grab disguised as service provision.

Huduma Namba required citizens to submit fingerprints, facial images, and detailed personal histories in order to be enrolled in state services. Yet the law governing how this data would be stored, used, and protected was passed only after mass registration was already underway. Public information campaigns were sparse. Opt-out mechanisms were non-existent. Courts eventually ruled that the rollout was unconstitutional in its original form, due to lack of legal safeguards. But by then, over 40 million Kenyans had already been captured in the system. The infrastructure of visibility had already been installed. The political utility of such a dataset—for policing, profiling, or population management—was no longer hypothetical.

Ghana followed a similar trajectory, albeit more quietly. Its national digital address system and biometric ID rollout, supported in part by international donors and tech contractors, was framed as an effort to formalise the informal economy. Indeed, many Ghanaians welcomed digital services that promised easier access to banking, taxation, and legal recognition. But what was not well communicated was the extent to which these systems would aggregate granular data on movement, location, and economic activity. Satellite imaging, mobile metadata, and address verification tools were stitched together to create a real-time map of the country's human geography. On paper, this improves planning. In practice, it builds a surveillance infrastructure that can be easily weaponised against dissent or deployed for social control.

Brazil's case reveals a more urbanised version of the same logic. Cities like São Paulo and Rio de Janeiro have adopted smart city technologies, ranging from intelligent traffic lights to predictive policing tools. One flagship project was the Centre of Operations Rio (COR), a high-tech command hub integrating feeds from thousands of cameras, sensors, and data points across the city. Initially conceived as a disaster response and traffic management system, COR quickly evolved into a tool for law enforcement and urban control. Facial recognition systems were trialled during Carnival under the pretext of locating fugitives. But civil liberties groups raised alarm about the normalisation of surveillance and the lack of transparency around how this data might be retained or shared.

These digital landgrabs share a common pattern: data infrastructure is implemented faster than legal or ethical frameworks can catch up. The population is told that these systems are for their own benefit—safer streets, faster services, better governance. Yet consent is rarely granular, revocable, or informed. Instead, it's bundled into platform terms of service, implied in citizenship duties, or embedded in state-corporate development agreements that are shielded from public scrutiny. Once these systems are operational, reversing them is politically and technically difficult. The "smart" city becomes the surveilled city. And its inhabitants are no longer just residents—they are data sources.

Crucially, these processes are not domestically driven alone. International donors, technology vendors, and consulting firms play a defining role. Whether it's the World Bank funding biometric registration, Chinese firms providing camera networks, or Western cloud providers hosting citizen data offshore, the architecture of digital governance is increasingly transnational. This raises a profound dilemma for sovereignty. Who owns the systems that know the population best? Who has the ability to audit, challenge, or halt their operation? And what happens when the companies building these systems are accountable not to voters, but to shareholders?

What makes this digital enclosure particularly effective is that it's often invisible. Unlike physical fences or checkpoints, data capture does not announce itself. Cameras are unmarked. Sensors are embedded. Consent is assumed. People participate in their own profiling by using mobile payment apps, accessing digital services, or simply walking through a sensor-equipped zone. The same infrastructure that allows for convenience—real-time traffic updates, mobile voting, digital ID access—also enables unprecedented control. And because it is embedded into everyday life, it ceases to be questioned.

Supporters argue that these systems modernise inefficient bureaucracies and provide marginalised populations with much-needed visibility. And in part, this is true. Informality, lack of documentation, and geographic exclusion are real challenges in many countries. But when inclusion comes at the cost of constant legibility, it becomes a double-edged sword. *Being seen by the state is not the same as being served by it.* The promise of digital development must be weighed against the risks of digitised domination.

It's also worth noting that digital landgrabs are not just about governments surveilling citizens. Private companies use these datasets to build predictive models, train AI systems, and extract behavioural patterns for commercial gain. In some cases, the same companies contracted to build national ID systems are also offering analytics products to insurers, advertisers, and security agencies. The citizen becomes not just a subject of governance, but a commodity—whose value is determined by their credit score, spending habits, or biometric traits. And the boundary between public infrastructure and private surveillance becomes increasingly blurred.

Resistance to these trends is growing, but remains fragmented. Legal challenges have occasionally succeeded in slowing down deployments or demanding greater transparency. Civil society groups in Kenya, Ghana, and Brazil have pushed for data protection laws and citizen oversight. But enforcement remains weak. And the sheer technical complexity of these systems means that meaningful accountability often requires specialised knowledge that few outside the architecture of implementation possess.

To address this imbalance, there must be a redefinition of what "consent" means in the context of infrastructure. A single checkbox during registration is not consent. Participating in society should not require submitting to permanent surveillance. Citizens must have the right to understand, contest, and opt out of systems that shape their visibility and access. Transparency must be proactive, not reactive. And digital development must be grounded in democratic deliberation, not technocratic convenience.

The old empires drew maps with borders. The new ones draw maps with data. The colonial cartographer is now an algorithm. And the conquest is silent, ambient, and automated. Understanding the dynamics of digital landgrabs means recognising that the battle for autonomy is no longer fought over land, but over *how people are seen.* It is not about ownership of territory, but of identity. And unless checked, this new form of colonisation may prove even harder to dismantle than the last.

Surveillance as Partnership

In the public imagination, surveillance is often associated with states—military agencies, authoritarian governments, and their secretive apparatuses.

But the reality of contemporary surveillance is neither purely governmental nor clearly visible. It is entangled in a web of partnerships, procurement deals, cloud infrastructure agreements, and software integrations that blur the lines between public interest and private ambition. *Surveillance today is not imposed; it is outsourced, monetised, and repackaged as progress.*

Under the pretext of modernisation, governments—particularly those with fragile democratic norms—are adopting surveillance tools developed not domestically, but by Western technology firms. In many cases, these tools are marketed through the language of innovation, security, or digital transformation. They promise efficiency and order. What they often deliver is control and opacity.

One of the clearest illustrations of this model is the relationship between Silicon Valley companies and authoritarian regimes. Technology firms—cloud service providers, facial recognition developers, AI analytics vendors—are increasingly operating as silent partners in national security. While governments manage the surface layer of law enforcement or social administration, the deeper layer of data collection, storage, and analysis is often delegated to private contractors whose incentives are shaped by market logic, not constitutional principles.

The core issue here is not simply that technology enables surveillance. It is that surveillance has become a byproduct of digital governance itself. When platforms become mediators of citizenship—when identity verification, education, healthcare, and communication flow through privately owned systems—then data extraction becomes structural, not incidental. And when that data flows across borders, into corporate servers located in liberal democracies, it creates a paradox: democratic infrastructure empowering undemocratic governance.

Consider the case of Saudi Arabia. In 2019, it was revealed that the state-run Absher app—available on both Apple's App Store and Google Play—was being used to allow male guardians to track and restrict the movements of women. While the app technically served as a portal for government services, its integration with visa and travel systems effectively enabled gender-based control, codified in software. International criticism was swift, but neither Apple nor Google removed the app. Their justification? The app complied with local laws. This abdication of ethical responsibility to national jurisdictions ignores the fact that these platforms *facilitate* the export of surveillance norms under the veneer of neutral service delivery.

A parallel case unfolded in the United Arab Emirates. The ToTok messaging app, which gained millions of users globally, was exposed by U.S. intelligence sources as a surveillance tool operated by the Emirati government. Marketed as a secure, free communication app, it was in fact used to harvest conversations, movements, and behavioural metadata. What enabled this deception was not just state strategy—it was the fact that app stores, cloud providers, and advertising ecosystems did not vet the true nature of the app before allowing it global reach. Again, surveillance was not enforced through brute force. It was distributed through platforms designed for convenience.

But these dynamics are not limited to the Gulf states. In Sub-Saharan Africa, Chinese surveillance exports have garnered substantial attention, but it is Western firms that often supply the software back-end or cloud infrastructure to support them. In Uganda, for example, Huawei helped install a city-wide surveillance camera network, ostensibly to reduce crime. But these cameras were later used to identify and detain political opposition figures during elections. The facial recognition components were provided through third-party software partners, some based in Europe and North America. Here again, surveillance was not sold as oppression. It was framed as capacity-building.

The logic of partnership allows all actors to deny accountability. Authoritarian regimes point to foreign companies as merely "technical vendors." Companies claim they are simply enabling government clients. Western intelligence agencies, meanwhile, benefit from the global telemetry made available by these partnerships—often through data-sharing agreements, contractor relationships, or legal loopholes around foreign data collection.

The Snowden revelations were pivotal in exposing how intelligence agencies such as the NSA developed covert pipelines for accessing data from U.S. technology companies. But what's changed since then is not the cessation of such activities. It's their legal and commercial integration. Cloud Act agreements, data localisation exemptions, and Five Eyes partnerships have made surveillance a multi-jurisdictional business. And once surveillance becomes business, it no longer requires political justification—just procurement paperwork.

This model has downstream consequences. For countries seeking loans, aid, or diplomatic favour, adopting Western-style digital identity systems or surveillance frameworks becomes a signalling mechanism. If they align their governance infrastructure with U.S. or EU technological norms, they may gain economic benefits. But those norms are not neutral. They embed specific architectures of legibility—systems for categorising, tracking, and filtering populations—that reflect the interests of their designers.

In this light, surveillance partnerships are not only bilateral—they are aspirational. Smaller states mimic the models of larger ones. Predictive policing in Chicago becomes a template for Lagos. Biometric border control in Australia is mirrored in Malaysia. And the rhetoric of "smart governance" allows every deployment to be framed as progress, regardless of its democratic consequences.

The most troubling development is the normalisation of surveillance under the rubric of digital public goods. Tools designed for crime prevention or health monitoring are being integrated into education, transportation, and welfare systems. Contact-tracing apps introduced during the pandemic, for instance, were marketed as temporary health measures. But in many cases, the infrastructure remained long after the emergency subsided. Taiwan, Singapore, and Israel each faced criticism for repurposing pandemic-era tools for law enforcement or immigration control. What begins as partnership in crisis becomes permanence by inertia.

Nor should we ignore the role of military and intelligence contractors in shaping this ecosystem. Firms such as Palantir, NSO Group, and Cellebrite operate at the intersection of counter-terrorism and commerce. They sell to both democratic and authoritarian clients, often with quiet government backing. Palantir, for example, has secured contracts with both ICE in the United States and health ministries abroad. Its platforms are pitched as data integration tools. But their power lies in connecting disparate data points into actionable intelligence—what might otherwise be called profiling.

Critics are often dismissed as alarmists. Companies insist on their adherence to local laws. Governments claim to use technology responsibly. But the lack of independent audits, the opacity of algorithmic processes, and the absence of citizen consent mechanisms reveal the structural imbalance. *Power is exercised not through spectacle, but through infrastructure.* The population sees the service; it does not see the system beneath.

A further danger lies in the way this model undermines democratic norms *at home*. When intelligence agencies collaborate with tech firms abroad, they often bring those capabilities back into domestic policing and governance. The tools developed for surveillance of foreign populations—mass metadata analysis, behavioural prediction, sentiment monitoring—become attractive options for managing internal dissent, immigration, or protest. The architecture of foreign surveillance returns through the back-door, repurposed for domestic control.

There is an urgent need to rethink the assumptions behind surveillance as partnership. When governments contract out core functions of visibility, they relinquish not just technical control, but democratic oversight. When firms claim neutrality in the face of oppression, they participate in its perpetuation. And when the public is excluded from decision-making about who sees them, how, and why, citizenship itself is diminished.

Surveillance is not just a matter of who watches—it's a question of *who defines visibility*. When that definition is outsourced, politicised, or hidden behind procurement jargon, the stakes are not just technical. They are existential. The citizen becomes a data point, the protester a risk score, the population a dashboard. And the promise of digital modernisation is revealed for what it often is: *a means of seeing, sorting, and silencing at scale.*

The challenge ahead is not simply to resist surveillance tools, but to expose the logic that enables them to be sold as solutions. That means demanding transparency not just from governments, but from the platforms, vendors, and consultants who make surveillance scalable. It means recognising that every modernisation initiative carries with it a politics of control. And it means reclaiming the idea that public safety and technological innovation are not incompatible with privacy—*unless we allow them to be.*

The Return of the Numbered Body

There is a long and often brutal history of turning human beings into data points. It predates silicon and servers, stretching back to colonial ledgers, slave registers, and internal pass systems. These systems did not merely record identity; they constructed it. They did not ask, "Who are you?" but answered instead, "Here is what you are—according to us." Today's biometric ID systems, for all their digital sophistication and sleek branding, inherit this logic. The body, once marked by shackles, tags, or ink, is now indexed by iris scans, facial vectors, and fingerprint hashes. And once again, the question resurfaces: *Who benefits when bodies are reduced to numbers?*

Historical cataloguing was not about inclusion. It was about administration. Slave registers in the British Caribbean detailed individuals not as people but as property—complete with inventory-style numbering and annotations about physical capacity, age, or market value. In apartheid South Africa, passbooks governed the movement of Black citizens, transforming daily mobility into a privilege contingent on state approval. In Nazi Germany, the tattooed numbers at Auschwitz were the final dehumanisation—a bureaucratic tool used to process mass death with cold efficiency. In each case, enumeration was not neutral. It was an instrument of control.

Biometric identity systems today claim to do the opposite. They promise empowerment, access, and visibility. They are sold as gateways to welfare, banking, and civic participation. Yet the architecture beneath them often remains disturbingly aligned with historical precedents. When a person must be scanned to be seen, measured to be counted, or databased to be recognised, the state is not merely identifying the citizen—it is defining the terms of existence itself.

Nigeria's National Identity Number (NIN) project illustrates both the promises and pitfalls of modern ID systems. Initially framed as a unifying effort to bring all Nigerians into the digital economy, the NIN programme quickly revealed its exclusionary dimensions. Millions of Nigerians found themselves locked out of basic services—including mobile communication and public benefits—simply because they had not completed the biometric enrolment. In rural areas, poor infrastructure made registration difficult. For marginalised communities, distrust in state systems created reluctance. Yet non-compliance was effectively punished through disconnection. The ID was not a tool for empowerment; it became a threshold of legitimacy.

Estonia's e-ID system, by contrast, is often celebrated as a model of digital citizenship. With a single credential, citizens can vote, bank, sign contracts, and access nearly all public services. The system is sleek, efficient, and widely accepted. But what is rarely discussed is how it embeds a deeper layer of programmability into everyday life. Each digital trace feeds into a wider surveillance infrastructure, one that consolidates behavioural patterns in the name of optimisation. The line between participation and surveillance grows thin. Visibility becomes conditional—not only on your actions, but on their alignment with the system's expectations.

This shift from identification to instrumentation is crucial. Biometric ID systems are not just about saying who someone is. They are about generating profiles, setting permissions, and filtering access. And once identity becomes programmable, behaviour follows. If your ID can expire, be suspended, or flagged—based on a score, suspicion, or bureaucratic anomaly—then identity becomes a mode of governance. Citizenship is no longer a status; it is a state of compliance.

In India, the Aadhaar system exemplifies this dynamic. The world's largest biometric database, Aadhaar links over a billion individuals to fingerprints and iris scans. It is used for welfare distribution, tax filings, school enrolment, and even private services like SIM card activation. The system has indeed streamlined service delivery. But it has also introduced new vectors of exclusion and coercion. Fingerprint mismatch can result in food denial. Identity theft becomes harder to detect, yet more damaging. And because the system is integrated into so many sectors, opting out is effectively impossible. Identity is no longer chosen; it is administered.

There is a particular risk when biometric systems are introduced in contexts of weak legal safeguards, minimal transparency, and limited digital literacy. In such environments, the body becomes a site of vulnerability. People do not fully understand what data is being collected, where it is stored, who accesses it, or for what purpose. Consent is rarely informed. Recourse is limited. And the institutional asymmetry—the distance between citizen and algorithm—makes contesting one's own identity nearly impossible.

What is often missing from policy discussions is the political economy of biometric infrastructure. These systems are not built in a vacuum. They are often funded by development banks, designed by Western firms, and rolled out in coordination with international aid agencies. The justification is usually framed as efficiency or inclusion. But inclusion *into what*, and under whose terms? If identity is linked to surveillance, if access is conditional, if digital credentials become instruments of behavioural regulation—then what we are witnessing is not inclusion, but enclosure.

The reduction of people to identifiers also shifts accountability. When systems fail, it is rarely the architects who are blamed. The individual is told they "did not register correctly," "entered the wrong PIN," or "missed the biometric match." Systemic breakdowns are reinterpreted as personal errors. This mirrors a much older pattern, where oppressed groups were blamed for their own exclusion. Today, that blame is automated, encoded into design, and distributed through platforms that appear impartial.

A further issue is the expansion of ID systems beyond state borders. International development agencies now require biometric verification for aid distribution. Refugees are scanned in camps. Migrants must submit to facial recognition. The logic is understandable—prevent fraud, streamline logistics. But the result is a global tracking system for the poor. Those already dispossessed are asked to surrender even more: their faces, their fingerprints, their digital shadows.

The commercial layer cannot be ignored. Biometric data is not just administratively valuable—it is commercially lucrative. Facial datasets fuel machine learning models. Behavioural logs train algorithms. Identity credentials feed financial products. What is harvested in the name of governance often ends up in the portfolios of private firms, sold as "anonymised data" but capable of re-identification. The person becomes the product. And the dignity of human identity is traded for efficiency gains and predictive insights.

There is also a cultural dimension. When identity is continuously measured, updated, or revoked, it shifts how people see themselves. Individuals begin to internalise the logic of monitoring. They curate behaviour to avoid friction. They defer to systems, even when those systems are opaque or unjust. The architecture of ID thus extends beyond the administrative—it enters the psychological. It becomes a form of soft compliance, where conformity is shaped not by force but by design.

This is not a call for rejecting identity systems altogether. IDs play a legitimate role in ensuring rights, access, and recognition. But the method and intent of their deployment matter deeply. A system designed to serve citizens should be accountable to them. It should be transparent, contestable, and respectful of dignity. When identity is imposed, unaccountable, or used to precondition access to basic life necessities, it ceases to be a tool of empowerment and becomes a mechanism of submission.

History is not simply repeating itself—it is being digitised. The shift from slave registers to biometric databases, from passbooks to facial recognition, is not just a technological upgrade. It is a reconfiguration of power. What was once enforced through paper and ink is now embedded in code and protocols. But the questions remain. Who controls the database? Who sets the criteria? And who is held accountable when the system excludes, misidentifies, or denies?

The numbered body is not a relic. It is a contemporary condition. To challenge it, we must do more than debate efficiency or fraud prevention. We must ask: *What kind of citizenship are we building when the path to recognition begins with a scan?* And who, in that transaction, gains power over whom?

Chapter 5

The Algorithmic Citizen

Citizenship is no longer defined solely by legal status, passports, or civic participation. Increasingly, it is computed. It is inferred from data, scored by systems, and enacted through code. To be recognised as a citizen in today's digital infrastructure is to be legible not just to the state, but to an expanding web of algorithmic intermediaries—platforms, databases, credit engines, and AI models. Eligibility for welfare, access to mobility, inclusion in political discourse—these are no longer exclusively determined by democratic institutions or constitutional guarantees. They are shaped, filtered, and often decided by algorithms whose logic remains opaque and whose accountability is diffuse. The algorithmic citizen is not just born or made; it is calculated.

This chapter maps how governance is increasingly outsourced to systems that compute rather than deliberate. The premise is seductive: data-driven decisions are faster, fairer, more consistent. But when government becomes an API and public services are reconfigured as platforms, the political contract is rewritten. What used to be a negotiation between citizen and state becomes a pattern-matching exercise between dataset and eligibility threshold. *Rights become recommendations.* Dignity becomes a variable. And justice, in many cases, is deferred—if not outright denied—by systems optimised for risk minimisation rather than human complexity.

Consider the quiet transformation of access. Housing applications in many cities now run through algorithms trained to evaluate "risk" profiles. Job-seekers are screened by predictive scoring tools long before a human reads their name. Loan decisions are made in milliseconds based on behavioural data harvested far beyond financial history: phone usage, social media habits, even keystroke rhythms. What emerges is not a transparent application process, but a computational wager on your probable reliability. The question is no longer *"Are you eligible?"* but *"Are you statistically safe enough to be worth including?"* This turns citizenship into conditionality—governed by pattern recognition, not deliberative justice.

The implications extend beyond welfare and into the heart of democratic life. Elections, once considered the sovereign ritual of civic expression, are now increasingly mediated—and in some cases, undermined—by digital infrastructure. From targeted voter suppression in the United States to full-scale internet blackouts in Myanmar, digital platforms are no longer neutral pipes. They are vectors of influence, capable of amplifying dissent or extinguishing it entirely. In Iran, encrypted apps are throttled during protests, while surveillance drones and facial recognition assist in pre-emptive arrests. In the European Union, the debate around content moderation, disinformation, and algorithmic curation has become central to the future of civic space. What these cases share is not geography or governance model, but a structural shift: civic engagement is increasingly conditional on algorithmic permission.

This is not merely a technical problem. It is a profound reconfiguration of democratic power. Historically, law served as the medium through which rights were articulated, contested, and enforced. Law had interpretation, delay, debate—friction that often served as a safeguard. Today, that friction is being engineered out. Predictive policing systems suggest where crimes *might* happen. AI sentencing tools "recommend" prison terms. Risk scoring in child welfare departments alerts case workers to "potential" neglect. In theory, these tools assist decision-makers. In practice, they set thresholds that are difficult to challenge. And once embedded, their authority hardens. The output of the algorithm becomes the rationale for the action. *Pre-justice replaces justice.*

The seduction of prediction lies in its promise of prevention. But prediction does not emerge from neutral ground. It is shaped by historical data, often reflecting past injustices and institutional biases. Predictive analytics cannot foresee the future; they automate the past. They do not eliminate bias; they scale it. The result is a feedback loop where existing inequities are reinforced under the guise of statistical rigour. A neighbourhood over-policed in the past is flagged as high-risk again. A family flagged for welfare fraud once is tagged for future monitoring. A school's poor performance history becomes a basis for reduced investment, ensuring decline continues. Predictive governance thus creates a form of bureaucratic fatalism—where the future is already accounted for, and deviation is discouraged.

And yet, these systems operate with astonishing opacity. Most algorithmic tools used in public administration are proprietary. Their code is protected. Their logic is not subject to public scrutiny. A citizen cannot cross-examine the model that denied their benefit or flagged their behaviour. There is no right to explanation, no forum for redress. This is a profound departure from democratic norms. In liberal democracies, law was expected to be visible, interpretable, challengeable. But when policy is embedded in code—executed instantly, invisibly, and at scale—the mechanisms of accountability begin to vanish. What does it mean to be governed by systems you cannot see, cannot question, and cannot escape?

This transformation also introduces a geopolitical dimension. Many of the tools now used for governance—facial recognition, sentiment analysis, predictive surveillance—are developed by a handful of private firms, mostly located in the United States and China. These firms are not democratically accountable. Yet they increasingly influence the design and enforcement of public policy across borders. When a company's machine learning system determines asylum eligibility in one country and content moderation rules in another, we are no longer dealing with national governance. We are confronting a new kind of regulatory empire—one defined by computational norms, economic incentives, and institutional opacity.

The architecture of algorithmic citizenship extends beyond national borders and into the core of legal meaning. When law is written as code, it ceases to be flexible. Legal language, for all its ambiguities and inefficiencies, allowed for negotiation, human discretion, and moral interpretation. Code, by contrast, is brittle. It is literal. It executes, regardless of nuance. A software-based tax rule does not understand unemployment, grief, or bureaucratic error. It applies rules without context. As more social contracts are translated into smart contracts, we are left with a version of legality that cannot bend, cannot listen, and cannot be persuaded. What results is not legal order—it is procedural absolutism.

At the heart of this chapter is a provocation: what does it mean to be a citizen in a world where rights are conditional on data profiles, civic participation is gated by platform protocols, and legal meaning is encoded into software you cannot amend? The algorithmic citizen is not a passive victim of systems. But nor are they an empowered agent in the traditional democratic sense. They navigate environments where choice is designed, where justice is forecasted, and where rights are recommended rather than guaranteed.

This chapter does not argue that algorithms have no place in governance. But it insists that their place must be interrogated. When eligibility becomes a probability score, when policy is filtered through infrastructure owned by private actors, and when code replaces debate as the medium of rule-making—we are not simply digitising government. We are redefining what governance is.

What follows in this chapter is an exploration of this redefinition. From healthcare algorithms that determine who receives treatment, to civic technologies that suppress or elevate protest, to predictive systems that reshape criminal justice and public policy—each section examines how algorithmic systems are quietly redrawing the lines of citizenship. These systems promise efficiency, precision, and scale. But they also introduce new forms of inequality, new sites of opacity, and new configurations of power.

The question is not whether we should automate public life. That process is already underway. The question is whether we can do so without abandoning the principles that made public life worth defending: transparency, dignity, accountability, and fairness. If we fail to ask these questions now, we risk a future in which rights are not denied outright—they are simply never calculated.

Rights by Recommendation

A growing number of decisions that once required human deliberation—welfare approval, loan qualification, housing allocation, medical triage—are now routed through algorithms. These systems do not merely support public service delivery; they increasingly *define* it. They filter applications, rank urgency, assess risk, and generate recommendations that are often treated as final decisions. What used to be rights—stable, universal, and anchored in law—are fast becoming recommendations: probabilistic permissions derived from pattern recognition. The shift is subtle, administrative in tone, and technocratic in presentation. But its implications for citizenship, equality, and justice are profound.

Public services have long been sites of social negotiation—spaces where needs meet resources, and where governments mediate competing claims on shared goods. Inserting algorithms into this space does not neutralise bias; it reconfigures power. What emerges is a system of governance in which *access is granted not by right, but by score.* Whether one receives housing, a student grant, or cancer treatment is increasingly determined by how well one's data conforms to statistical models of worthiness, need, or compliance. The logic is actuarial, not civic. And while efficiency may improve in the short term, the long-term erosion of procedural fairness and public trust is a price quietly exacted.

Nowhere is this transformation more apparent than in the welfare state. In the Netherlands, the SyRI (System Risk Indication) project exemplified the ambitions of data-driven eligibility checks. Designed to detect welfare fraud, SyRI pooled data from multiple agencies—employment records, tax filings, housing details—and fed it into a proprietary risk-scoring model. Neighbourhoods were assigned fraud risk scores, which then informed caseworker interventions. Crucially, those targeted were given no insight into how their data was used, nor any meaningful recourse to contest the algorithmic assessment. In 2020, a Dutch court ruled SyRI unconstitutional, citing a violation of privacy and lack of transparency. Yet similar systems continue to operate in various guises across Europe and beyond, rebranded as "efficiency tools" or "smart governance."

In the United States, algorithmic scoring systems have been deployed to manage access to housing vouchers. The Allegheny Family Screening Tool, used in Pennsylvania's child welfare system, assigns risk scores to families based on historical data, flagging them for further investigation. While the tool is designed to assist rather than replace human judgment, research has shown that social workers often defer to the model's outputs, especially under caseload pressure. Moreover, these systems are trained on historical data rife with racial and socioeconomic bias. As a result, they risk encoding discrimination into future decision-making—even as they operate under the banner of fairness.

Healthcare presents another frontier for algorithmic eligibility. During the COVID-19 pandemic, hospitals in the United Kingdom and United States developed triage algorithms to allocate limited ICU resources. One such model, developed by a major health tech company, prioritised patients based on survival probability, underlying conditions, and age. In theory, this ensured a rational distribution of care. In practice, it meant that certain groups—especially disabled individuals and those with complex health needs—were deprioritised by default. These patients were not explicitly denied care, but their data profiles rendered them less "viable" in the eyes of the algorithm. The model may have been statistically sound, but its moral calculus was invisible, and its consequences irreversible.

Credit scoring has followed a similar path. Traditional credit histories are increasingly supplemented—or replaced—by alternative data: utility payments, social media behaviour, GPS location patterns. In China, the integration of financial data with behavioural metrics has culminated in the Social Credit System, where creditworthiness extends to civic virtue. But the trend is not limited to authoritarian regimes. In the U.S., start-ups like Zest AI and Upstart tout the use of machine learning to offer "fairer" loan assessments, claiming their models uncover hidden potential in applicants overlooked by traditional scoring. Yet these same models can penalise people for living in the "wrong" postcode, having "inconsistent" employment, or even making frequent phone calls at night—patterns the system interprets as risk indicators. The result is an opaque financial sieve, where access to credit is framed as a service, not a right, and where the reasoning behind rejection is rarely intelligible.

Mobility, too, is being filtered through algorithmic gates. Ride-sharing companies routinely ban drivers and riders based on opaque safety scores. Airlines use predictive systems to flag passengers for additional screening, often without evidence or explanation. Visa applications are increasingly evaluated by algorithmic triage systems that sort applicants into low- and high-risk categories based on travel history, demographics, and social connections. The border becomes not just a physical checkpoint, but a computational decision zone—where access is conditional on digital profiles built long before the traveller arrives.

At the heart of these systems lies a fundamental shift in how need is recognised and how responsibility is assigned. Algorithms assess probability, not context. They infer intention, not explain behaviour. This introduces a double erasure: individuals are abstracted into datasets, and those datasets are judged against normative baselines that are rarely made explicit. Who sets the thresholds? Who audits the assumptions? Who is accountable when a recommendation becomes a denial?

Proponents argue that algorithmic recommendations reduce human bias, streamline bureaucracy, and deliver services more efficiently. There is some merit to this view. Well-designed systems can uncover hidden patterns, flag errors, and process complex datasets that would overwhelm human administrators. In theory, they can surface new insights and deliver targeted interventions. But the key term here is *well-designed*—and in most public deployments, design is constrained by budget, vendor secrecy, and institutional inertia. The result is a proliferation of black-box systems that lack transparency, meaningful oversight, or mechanisms for appeal.

Moreover, the reliance on historical data as a predictive tool introduces a paradox. The very datasets used to build these models are artefacts of past policy choices, shaped by systemic inequalities. When fed into algorithms, they create a self-reinforcing loop: groups historically marginalised are flagged as high-risk, subjected to greater scrutiny, and disproportionately denied access. The system then uses these outcomes to refine its model, further entrenching the patterns it was meant to overcome.

Transparency alone cannot fix this. Even if source code were open and datasets available, most users lack the expertise or time to audit complex machine learning models. What is needed is *accountable design*—systems built with procedural safeguards, human review pathways, and institutional checks that go beyond superficial fairness metrics. Equally crucial is *democratic design*: public participation in deciding when and where algorithmic tools should be used, and under what constraints.

The current model often bypasses these considerations altogether. Procurement decisions are made behind closed doors. Vendors claim proprietary rights over model logic. Policymakers are seduced by cost savings and digital dashboards. Citizens, meanwhile, encounter the system only when it fails them—when benefits are denied, services withheld, or appeals ignored. And because these systems operate at scale, the damage is often silent, cumulative, and disproportionately borne by those with the least ability to contest it.

This new architecture of eligibility reshapes not only access, but identity. People begin to tailor their behaviour to align with algorithmic expectations. Welfare recipients avoid certain purchases that might trigger fraud alerts. Jobseekers adjust their CVs to match keyword filters. Loan applicants modify online habits to preserve their credit score. Public life becomes a game of optimisation—where the goal is not authenticity, but algorithmic legibility. What emerges is a form of soft coercion: not enforced by law, but incentivised by code.

This raises a deeper question about the nature of rights in a digital society. If access to healthcare, housing, and finance depends on behavioural prediction, then rights become conditional on compliance with statistical norms. The danger is not merely exclusion—it is the quiet dismantling of the idea that public services are owed, rather than granted. That they are entitlements, not privileges. That they are grounded in shared humanity, not personal data profiles.

Algorithmic recommendations can support human decision-making. But they must not replace it. To preserve the integrity of public services, we must ensure that rights remain rights—not probabilities filtered through corporate infrastructure and mathematical abstractions. The challenge is not technical; it is political. Who gets to decide what counts as "normal" behaviour? Who defines risk, and for whom? And when the system is wrong—as it inevitably will be—who bears the cost?

In the end, rights by recommendation are not rights at all. They are offers, contingent on invisible calculations and unexamined thresholds. If we are to safeguard the promise of equal access, we must demand systems that respect not only efficiency, but dignity. Not only outcomes, but process. And not only accuracy, but accountability. The future of public service delivery will be digital. But whether it remains just—that is still a choice.

Democracy's API

In the age of digitisation, democracy has acquired an interface. Not a metaphorical one—a literal set of digital gates, endpoints, and permissions through which civic engagement increasingly flows. Like an API in software, democracy is now mediated by platforms, protocols, and code, where access and visibility are contingent on the rules set by gatekeepers. These rules are rarely discussed in public debate, but their impact is profound: *who gets heard, who gets seen, and who gets silenced is increasingly determined by systems never voted on, owned by entities never elected.*

Whether in authoritarian regimes, fragile democracies, or advanced liberal states, elections, protests, and public discourse are no longer governed only by law and constitution—they are governed by code. That code is written by platform engineers, app developers, and intelligence contractors, not parliamentarians or constitutional lawyers. This shift reframes democratic participation as a function of *system compatibility.* If your protest doesn't reach the network, if your opposition party's livestream is throttled, if your political ad is demoted by an algorithm—did it really happen? In this architecture, dissent can be filtered, fragmented, or flagged without overt censorship. The result is a democracy that appears intact on paper, but is quietly reshaped by infrastructure.

Myanmar offers an unambiguous case study. After a decade of fragile democratic opening, the military coup of February 2021 triggered mass resistance—much of it digital. Protesters organised on Facebook, live-streamed rallies, and documented military abuses in real time. The junta responded with systematic internet blackouts, DNS throttling, and mobile app bans. These were not random outages—they were targeted disruptions aimed at disabling coordination and crushing dissent. Even as the world condemned the coup, tech platforms complied with legal takedown requests from the regime, citing policy neutrality. In effect, the infrastructure of connection became a weapon of suppression. The public square collapsed into a loading screen.

In Iran, the dynamics are more cyclical but no less controlled. Each wave of protest—2009, 2017, 2019, 2022—has been met with a calibrated digital crackdown. Authorities slow the internet to sub-2G speeds, block messaging apps like Signal and Telegram, and deploy deep packet inspection tools to monitor traffic. More recently, they've introduced the "National Information Network"—an isolated intranet that mimics global platforms but remains under state control. It is designed to keep the population online *and* under surveillance. Platforms like Instagram, one of the few remaining Western services accessible in Iran, have become battlegrounds—where activists' accounts are removed, shadow-banned, or targeted by bot swarms pushing regime propaganda. Protest still exists, but it does so in constant negotiation with code—contorting itself around API limits, encryption loopholes, and platform policy changes.

Contrast this with the European Union, where the infrastructure of civic control is subtler, but no less consequential. EU institutions have championed digital rights on paper, passing laws such as the General Data Protection Regulation (GDPR) and the Digital Services Act (DSA). Yet these frameworks also open the door to new forms of moderation, filtering, and content ranking that can easily be leveraged against dissent under the guise of combating disinformation. During the COVID-19 pandemic, for example, the European Commission worked closely with major platforms to suppress "harmful content," including criticism of government lockdowns and vaccine policy. While some of this was warranted, much of it operated in the grey zone between moderation and censorship—where terms of service effectively replaced public deliberation.

The problem is not surveillance alone. It is the fusion of surveillance with policy enforcement, where predictive analytics and content scoring are used to pre-emptively manage civic life. Facebook's political ad algorithm determines which demographics see which messages, subtly shaping campaign reach and resonance. Google's search engine decides which opposition party's manifesto is more "relevant." Twitter's trending tab influences the salience of protest hashtags. These decisions are not made by humans in real time—they are outputs of recommendation engines designed to maximise engagement, not fairness. Civic discourse becomes collateral damage in a business model optimised for velocity and virality.

The 2016 U.S. election and the Brexit referendum both exposed the extent to which political processes could be shaped by targeted messaging, behavioural profiling, and algorithmic amplification. Yet the lessons from those events have not been adequately absorbed. Today's platforms are larger, their reach deeper, and their predictive capacity greater. Political microtargeting continues largely unchecked, as does the use of bots and astroturf campaigns to simulate public consensus. What looks like democratic debate may in fact be an echo of engineered outrage—calibrated for maximum polarisation.

One might argue that democracies are resilient—that people adapt, laws evolve, and technology is neutral. But neutrality is a myth in infrastructure. Every design choice—what is amplified, throttled, flagged, or ignored—reflects implicit priorities. When digital platforms control the means of assembly, the *rules of association change.* You may have the right to protest, but not the bandwidth. You may have the right to speak, but not to be heard. The API does not block speech; it demotes it, delays it, or buries it beneath layers of algorithmic noise.

Activists and civil society groups have responded with creativity—using VPNs, mesh networks, encrypted apps, and mirror sites to circumvent blockades. But these are tactical responses to structural constraints. The broader question is institutional: *who governs digital space, and on whose behalf?* The current answer is a patchwork of platform policy teams, state regulators, and private security firms. None are democratically elected, and few are accountable to the public. The architecture of civic life has been outsourced—not just to the private sector, but to entities whose incentives rarely align with democratic transparency.

This poses a particular challenge for marginalised groups. Surveillance and moderation disproportionately affect those already excluded from mainstream political discourse—minorities, dissidents, asylum seekers, whistleblowers. Their voices are more likely to trigger algorithmic suspicion, be flagged as "unusual," or fall foul of vague platform guidelines. The result is not just suppression, but *invisibility*—a form of erasure that is difficult to prove and harder to reverse. When democracy is mediated through APIs, *those least legible to the system are most easily excluded from it.*

Rebuilding democratic resilience requires more than regulating platform behaviour. It demands rethinking the underlying architecture—how digital public space is built, maintained, and governed. This includes designing alternative infrastructures: publicly accountable platforms, open-source civic tools, and decentralised communication networks that respect both privacy and pluralism. It also requires transparency at the level of code: algorithmic audits, participatory policy-making, and enforceable rights over how civic data is used. These are not technical luxuries—they are democratic necessities.

Ultimately, the question is not whether technology is good or bad for democracy. That binary is too crude. The real issue is *who controls the in-*

terface. Today, democracy's API is proprietary, opaque, and asymmetrically governed. Until that changes, elections may still be held, protests still mounted, and civic rituals still performed. But their meaning will be increasingly conditional—filtered not by law, but by protocol. And in that filtering lies the quiet erosion of the democratic promise.

Predictive Governance

The most radical transformation in state power over the last decade has not been the expansion of surveillance or the rise of digital identification. It is the quiet shift from retrospective governance to anticipatory control—from responding to what has happened, to attempting to manage what *might* happen. Predictive governance promises efficiency, security, and pre-emption. But behind this promise lies a redefinition of justice itself: *no longer a response to harm, but a set of probabilities assigned to behaviour before it occurs.*

Across jurisdictions, from Chicago to Shenzhen, predictive analytics now inform how governments allocate risk, determine intent, and direct public resources. Risk scores are applied to individuals, neighbourhoods, and entire communities. These scores are built not on clear evidence of wrongdoing, but on correlations: past arrests, social connections, school attendance, credit history, internet searches. The data is real, but the judgments derived from it are inferential—an algorithmic logic that increasingly substitutes for legal reasoning.

Predictive policing is the most visible frontier of this shift. Systems like PredPol in the United States, or the Skynet platform used in parts of China, process historical crime data to forecast where crimes are likely to occur and who might commit them. Police officers are then dispatched to these locations—not because a crime is in progress, but because the algorithm suggests risk. The logic is actuarial. Just as insurers price policies based on risk profiles, law enforcement now targets citizens based on statistical likelihood. The result is a form of *pre-justice*: action taken in anticipation of harm, not in response to it.

This model has profound implications for democratic accountability. In traditional legal frameworks, rights are universal and violations are adjudicated after the fact. Under predictive systems, rights become conditional—granted or constrained based on an individual's forecasted behaviour. A student flagged as "at-risk" may be placed under additional surveillance. A resident in a "high-risk" neighbourhood may experience more frequent police encounters. In both cases, the trigger is not conduct, but categorisation. *Your future has been scored, and the state has decided to act upon it.*

The problem is compounded by opacity. Predictive models are often proprietary, their parameters protected as trade secrets. Individuals cannot contest a score they cannot see, produced by variables they do not understand. The principle of due process erodes in such a system. One cannot appeal an outcome whose logic is hidden, nor can one prove innocence against a probability.

In 2016, the ProPublica investigation into COMPAS, a risk-assessment tool used in U.S. courts to inform bail and sentencing decisions, revealed stark racial disparities. Black defendants were far more likely to be labelled as high-risk than white defendants with similar criminal histories. The developers of COMPAS argued that the system was "fair" because its overall predictive accuracy was balanced across groups. But this obscured a critical ethical divide: *fairness by outcome* versus *fairness by impact*. A model can be statistically fair and socially unjust, particularly when it amplifies existing inequalities.

Europe has not been immune to the lure of pre-emption. In the Netherlands, the SyRI system (System Risk Indication) was deployed to detect welfare fraud by integrating data from multiple government agencies—employment records, education, taxes, housing. Residents of certain postal codes were flagged as suspicious and subjected to investigation. The criteria were never publicly disclosed. In 2020, a Dutch court ruled the system illegal, citing violations of human rights and data protection laws. But for years, it had already reshaped how the welfare state treated its most vulnerable citizens: not as clients, but as threats to be managed.

India provides a parallel story, though rooted in a different socio-political context. The Aadhaar biometric ID system, originally introduced to improve public service delivery, has increasingly been linked to predictive models of subsidy eligibility. Algorithms rank citizens by their likelihood of fraud, their consumption history, or their income volatility. A low score can result in being excluded from food rations, housing assistance, or school enrolments—not through overt denial, but through technical "errors" in authentication or eligibility. The system need not accuse you of wrongdoing; it simply fails to recognise your right to be seen.

What unites these examples is not just the use of predictive analytics, but the ideology underpinning them. They embody a managerial vision of governance, where uncertainty is the problem and statistical control is the solution. In this vision, citizens are no longer political subjects but *data subjects*—understood primarily through patterns, anomalies, and risk profiles. Governance becomes less about law and more about logistics: optimising flows, reducing friction, managing deviations.

Proponents argue that such tools improve efficiency, reduce human bias, and enable better resource allocation. There is some truth in that. But it ignores a deeper cost: *the procedural and moral foundations of justice are bypassed.* Pre-emptive logic does not just inform decisions—it replaces them. When predictive systems shape school admissions, welfare disbursement, or policing routes, they effectively *write policy in code*, without parliamentary debate or judicial oversight.

Moreover, predictive governance alters the citizen's relationship with the state. Trust is no longer built through transparency or fairness, but through compliance and legibility. You must be seen in the right data sets, behave in expected ways, and minimise anomalies in order to receive your rights. This produces what some legal scholars have called "informational conformity"—the pressure to act in ways that are algorithmically unremarkable. The quieter you are in the data, the safer you are from intervention.

This has chilling effects on activism, dissent, and community organising—particularly among minority groups already subject to heightened scrutiny. In cities like Los Angeles and Chicago, gang databases and social media monitoring tools have been used to flag youth as "affiliated" based on music preferences, clothing, or network connections. Once flagged, even a minor infraction can lead to disproportionate sanctions. The system is not designed to understand intent—it is designed to flag deviation.

Importantly, the shift to predictive governance is not limited to security or welfare. It is rapidly extending into urban planning, health policy, and climate response. Smart city platforms, such as those piloted in Singapore, Dubai, and parts of Canada, rely on real-time data to allocate resources and adjust policy in dynamic ways. This can yield efficiencies—optimising traffic, managing energy use, allocating emergency services. But the underlying logic remains: decisions are made not by deliberation, but by prediction. The citizen becomes a variable in a simulation, not a participant in a polity.

This raises foundational questions: *Can a democracy function when the future is pre-decided by code?* What happens to accountability when no human takes responsibility for an outcome, because the algorithm "said so"? And who controls the models—who decides what outcomes are desirable, what risks are unacceptable, and what correlations are permissible?

There are no easy answers. But one thing is clear: predictive governance is not merely a tool. It is a *mode of power*—one that shifts the terms of legitimacy from law to likelihood. As governments adopt this model, often with little public debate, they are not just upgrading bureaucracy. They are *rewriting the social contract.*

To engage seriously with the future of democracy, we must interrogate the architecture of prediction. That means demanding transparency in models, meaningful consent in data use, and institutional safeguards that preserve due process. But more than that, it means reaffirming a political principle that no algorithm can override: *justice is not a probability score.* It is a right—earned, upheld, and protected not by prediction, but by deliberation and law. When that distinction is lost, governance becomes not more efficient, but more dangerous. It no longer serves society—it calculates it.

Code as Constitution

Few people pause to consider that software code—the invisible architecture underpinning our digital lives—now functions as a kind of law. Not metaphorically, but materially. It determines what we can access, how we behave, and which outcomes are permissible. Unlike traditional law, which is debated, interpreted, and amended through visible democratic mechanisms, code is enforced automatically, silently, and often without recourse. *When governance migrates into software, legal authority migrates with it—but without the safeguards.*

Modern constitutions were designed to place limits on power. They enshrined checks and balances, ensured rights could not be arbitrarily revoked, and bound rulers to rule within law. But when legal authority is expressed through algorithms—when eligibility, compliance, and enforcement are encoded into digital systems—the balance between citizens and institutions begins to tilt. *The rules still exist. They're just no longer negotiated in public.*

Consider social media platforms, which now mediate much of the public sphere. Their content moderation systems are not administered by elected judges or regulated bodies but by proprietary algorithms. These systems determine who gets seen, who gets silenced, and which narratives rise to prominence. Speech is not outlawed in any formal legal sense, but it is filtered, downranked, and often erased without explanation. The platform doesn't need to issue a warrant. It simply tweaks the code.

This is not a debate about censorship; it is a shift in the *location* of power. Platform rules—whether about hate speech, misinformation, or political content—are enforced through machine logic rather than human judgment. The terms of enforcement are not publicly deliberated. They are written into back-end systems, refined in secret, and deployed globally. In this model, *code does not merely reflect policy—it is policy.*

Take Apple's AirDrop feature in China. In 2022, after its use by protesters to share political messages, Apple quietly reduced the default exposure window for receiving content from "Everyone" to "10 minutes," and only for devices sold in China. No law was passed. No regulation was debated. One software update, rolled out in silence, altered the balance of power between citizens and the state. *That is the constitutional effect of code: it redraws rights without asking.*

Financial systems provide another striking example. Programmable money—especially Central Bank Digital Currencies—can embed conditions directly into the currency itself. Funds can be made to expire, to function only in certain sectors, or to freeze based on risk flags. These are not theoretical features; they are being piloted in multiple countries. And once coded, they do not require legislative intervention. The law is not interpreted. It is executed.

Such systems offer technical efficiency and policy precision. But they also bypass procedural safeguards. A traditional law can be challenged in court, revised through protest, or amended through election. *A smart contract cannot be negotiated—it executes automatically.* And while one might appeal a legal sentence, one cannot appeal a line of code that has already denied you access, blocked your transaction, or labelled you ineligible.

This is particularly evident in welfare systems. In the UK, the rollout of Universal Credit was paired with algorithmic assessments of eligibility and fraud risk. Decisions that were once made by caseworkers—who could exercise discretion—are now handled by data-matching systems. Errors, once rectifiable by explanation, become Kafkaesque cycles of rejection because the logic is hidden. The appeal process, where it exists, often lacks transparency and is divorced from any clear account of the decision-making path.

Once law becomes code, its mutability—once a virtue of democratic governance—turns into rigidity. Software is difficult to change quickly. Even well-intentioned reforms lag behind technological deployment. When public systems are built by outsourced contractors, or when terms are dictated by multinational vendors, democratic accountability is further diluted. Who is responsible when the code fails? Who is liable when a system punishes the wrong person? More often than not, the answer is *no one*. Blame disperses across technical departments, procurement contracts, and black-box systems. Responsibility evaporates.

The global nature of digital infrastructure further complicates matters. Tech platforms do not operate within the borders of single states. They function as transnational actors with jurisdictional flexibility. When Facebook enforces a content policy, it does so in Nigeria and Norway alike. When Google tweaks its search algorithm, the effects ripple across elections, economies, and education. These decisions, though made by private entities, have public consequences. Yet unlike nation-states, they are not accountable to parliaments, courts, or civil society. They are accountable to users only to the extent that users generate revenue.

And yet, the state is not a bystander in this transformation. Governments increasingly outsource governance to code. Whether in the form of automated surveillance, digital identity systems, or predictive analytics, states are embracing code not as a supplement to law but as its substitute. The Indian government's Aadhaar system—a biometric ID linked to welfare, taxation, and health—is a legal infrastructure, but it is also a computational one. Your rights within that system are determined not by statute but by the functioning of databases, servers, and verification protocols. If the system fails, your existence as a legal person is suspended.

There is a deeper cultural shift beneath this architectural change. Code, unlike law, is not written for interpretation. It is written for execution. There is no ambiguity, no room for dissent. This binary logic—true or false, access granted or denied—erodes the deliberative space that justice requires. Human judgment, with its imperfections and empathy, is increasingly displaced by algorithmic finality.

Some have argued that the answer lies in greater transparency—open-source code, audit logs, or explainable AI. These are necessary but insufficient. *Transparency is not the same as accountability.* A system may be open and still unchallengeable. It may be legible to experts but inaccessible to those it governs. The deeper issue is legitimacy. Who gets to write the rules? Whose interests are served in their execution? And what happens when those rules are embedded not in constitutions but in systems no one voted for?

To confront these questions, we must resist the tendency to treat code as neutral. Code is written by people, funded by institutions, and deployed within political contexts. Every design choice is a normative decision: what to include, what to exclude, what to prioritise. And once those decisions are deployed at scale, their effects become constitutive. They shape not only what is possible, but what is *permissible.*

The future of democratic governance depends on our ability to distinguish between *rule by law* and *rule by code.* The former invites contestation, argument, revision. The latter imposes outcomes by logic gates. If we accept the drift toward algorithmic constitutionalism without scrutiny, we risk waking up in societies where rights are no longer protected, only processed—and where justice is no longer interpreted, only executed.

Chapter 6

Control in the Language of Care

The most effective forms of control are not those that threaten, but those that reassure. When surveillance arrives cloaked in safety, when coercion is wrapped in compassion, and when biometric checkpoints are framed as instruments of inclusion, resistance becomes more difficult—not because the systems are less invasive, but because they sound like help. *Modern governance is learning to speak in the grammar of care. The question is whether we are still listening critically.*

This chapter explores how the aesthetics of benevolence—health, safety, inclusion, dignity—are increasingly used to legitimise highly centralised systems of monitoring, behavioural conditioning, and digital dependency. These initiatives do not declare themselves as instruments of power. Instead, they are sold as tools for empowerment. Yet scratch beneath the surface and the architecture is one of conditionality, surveillance, and asymmetrical decision-making.

During the COVID-19 pandemic, for instance, the rapid rollout of vaccine passports was justified not through threats, but through appeals to public responsibility and mutual protection. Opting out wasn't framed as an expression of bodily autonomy, but as a failure of solidarity. The message was subtle yet forceful: responsible citizens comply. But once these systems were in place—QR-based check-ins, Bluetooth contact tracing, immunisation databases—their potential use extended far beyond the original emergency. *Temporary infrastructure built for health has a curious habit of lingering.* What begins as a measure to "protect the vulnerable" can quickly become the scaffolding for long-term digital gatekeeping.

Health surveillance is not the only domain where care becomes a conduit for control. In development contexts, biometric ID systems are routinely rolled out under the banner of inclusion. Programmes like India's Aadhaar or Kenya's Huduma Namba are presented as solutions to statelessness and inequality. Governments and NGOs argue that a digital identity enables access to welfare, banking, and education. But these IDs do not merely *enable* access—they often *define* it. The logic is conditional: no ID, no benefits. Once tethered to public services, biometric systems can easily become levers of exclusion. The promise of dignity becomes a justification for digitised dependency. *What looks like access is often just compliance by another name.*

Such initiatives are rarely introduced as authoritarian tools. Quite the opposite—they are marketed as humanitarian breakthroughs. Digital inclusion for the poor. Targeted cash transfers for the needy. Smart subsidies to reduce fraud. Every word in this lexicon is carefully selected to frame the system as a moral good. But as we will explore in this chapter, *intent does not equal outcome.* A programme designed to help the poor can just as easily be used to discipline them. A policy intended to enhance public health can quietly normalise real-time surveillance. *The rhetoric of compassion can obscure the architecture of control.*

Take the rise of conditional cash transfer (CCT) programmes and basic income pilots. Many of these initiatives are now fused with biometric verification and behavioural nudging. In Brazil, families receiving Bolsa Família funds must ensure their children attend school and get vaccinated—monitored by data systems. In Kenya, some digital welfare pilots experiment with mobile money disbursements contingent on geolocation or usage data. These are not necessarily malevolent in design. But they are profoundly consequential in structure. *They reshape the relationship between state and citizen—from one rooted in entitlement to one structured by performance metrics.*

Even more subtly, we are witnessing the emergence of what might be called the *infantilised citizen.* The individual is no longer seen as a rational actor capable of moral judgement, but as a subject to be guided, nudged, and managed. Public policy borrows from behavioural economics and platform design. Governments use push notifications, colour-coded alerts, and automated messaging to "encourage" desirable behaviours. The model is less about enforcement and more about steering—an architecture of soft coercion that feels intuitive but is deeply asymmetrical. *The citizen becomes the object of governance, not its co-author.*

This infantilisation is reinforced by digital interfaces that mediate every interaction. Consider how welfare recipients are now required to interact with app-based systems that track their activities, enforce compliance conditions, and deliver decisions without human explanation. Appeals processes are outsourced to algorithms. The logic is managerial, not democratic. And while these systems often *work*—in the narrow sense of fraud reduction or administrative efficiency—they fundamentally alter the moral contract of the state. *Care becomes contingent. Autonomy becomes optional.*

To critique these developments is not to deny the value of health, safety, or inclusion. The point is not to reject the language of care, but to interrogate its uses. Who defines what counts as care? Who decides the conditions under which it is delivered? And what happens when those definitions are embedded in code, enforced by infrastructure, and insulated from accountability?

These are not abstract concerns. As this chapter will demonstrate, the convergence of humanitarian rhetoric and digital infrastructure has material consequences. It determines who receives a benefit, who is deemed a risk, and who remains invisible to the system altogether. When the logic of benevolence replaces the logic of rights, scrutiny weakens. When citizens are treated as clients to be served, rather than participants to be heard, dissent becomes a form of ingratitude. *And when control is expressed through care, resistance becomes harder to articulate—let alone organise.*

The chapters that follow will examine these dynamics in concrete detail. We will unpack how biometric welfare systems, digital identity regimes, and behavioural nudging are not merely policy tools but expressions of a deeper shift: from citizen to subject, from entitlement to eligibility, from rights to rewards. You will encounter examples from health ministries to fintech pilots, from social safety nets to algorithmic moral scoring. Each case illustrates a broader transformation in governance—*where control no longer needs to look like coercion. It can wear the face of kindness and still hold a firm grip.*

The task, then, is to develop the intellectual and civic discipline to read between the lines. To see when a safety net is also a snare. To ask whether inclusion demands submission. And to remember that true care is not merely about protection, but about respecting the capacity of people to govern themselves. When governance speaks the language of care, the citizen must listen closely—not for comfort, but for consent.

Benevolent Tyranny

Few tools of control are more effective than those introduced as acts of protection. When state surveillance is sold as public health, when movement restrictions are framed as civic duty, and when emergency alerts evolve into digital compliance checks, the boundary between governance and paternalism begins to blur. Control does not always arrive cloaked in fear;

sometimes, it arrives in the language of care, framed as common sense, backed by experts, and delivered through platforms we already trust. The more comfortable the interface, the more invisible the intrusion.

The global response to the COVID-19 pandemic offered a real-time case study in how liberal democracies and authoritarian states alike adopted highly centralised systems of behavioural enforcement—less through mandates and more through moral framing. Vaccine passports became the entry point for a broader societal infrastructure of conditional access. Whether to board a train, enter a school, or access public services, individuals were required to show proof of compliance. These systems were defended as temporary, essential, and scientifically grounded. Yet in many jurisdictions, the technical architecture outlived the initial crisis, finding new utility in unrelated domains. *The crisis normalised the infrastructure; the infrastructure enabled a new normal.*

Emergency management technologies, traditionally limited to disaster warnings, have expanded into tools of behavioural notification. Public health alerts, curfews, climate warnings, and "community safety" messages are now frequently pushed via SMS, apps, and real-time location systems. These tools are lauded for their efficiency, but they operate on asymmetrical terms: the user can receive, but not question; comply, but not negotiate. The act of being notified becomes the precursor to being monitored. *Consent becomes implied, not granted.*

The power of this shift lies in its psychological alignment with trust. Public health has long been one of the most credible domains of state activity. By embedding surveillance functions within that credibility, governments have expanded their operational reach without the social friction typical of traditional law enforcement. For instance, digital contact tracing apps in countries like Singapore (TraceTogether) and Australia (COVIDSafe) were launched with voluntary framing but later expanded through integration with public venue check-ins and workplace mandates. The technology was opt-in only until participation became a de facto requirement for public life. *The language of public good concealed a quiet recalibration of citizen-state relations.*

Beyond health, the rhetorical device of *inclusion* has emerged as a dominant justification for expanding digital infrastructure with coercive capabilities. Initiatives aimed at "connecting the unconnected" often involve registering biometric identities, linking them to state platforms, and conditioning access to welfare on behavioural compliance. In theory, these systems are empowering. In practice, they tether participation in public life to state-controlled identifiers. When inclusion depends on enrolment in surveillance systems, the very notion of empowerment is inverted. What is framed as access becomes a form of oversight. *Being counted is not always the same as being seen.*

This architecture becomes more potent when combined with algorithmic enforcement. For instance, in China, the health QR code system initially developed for pandemic management continues to govern mobility across provinces. A green code allows movement; a red one restricts it. The user often has no transparency into why their status changes or how long the restriction will last. Such systems are technically precise but procedurally opaque—an inversion of democratic accountability. They reduce law to interface and discretion to code. *Authority no longer needs a badge when it has an app.*

Western democracies, while less explicit in enforcement, have mirrored many of these trends. In the United Kingdom, debates over digital immunity certificates stirred concern not only about privacy but about function creep—where health-related credentials could be linked with other domains such as travel history, employment eligibility, or financial access. The infrastructure built to manage a virus is neither neutral nor temporary. Its future applications may lie beyond public health—possibly in law enforcement, immigration, or welfare eligibility. *Every new function becomes easier to justify once the system is accepted as necessary.*

This is the essence of benevolent tyranny: a structure of control that elicits compliance not through fear, but through the appearance of care. It is a governance model that asks not what is permitted, but what is "safe," "wise," or "socially responsible." It shifts the moral burden to the citizen. Noncompliance is no longer framed as dissent but as selfishness, recklessness, or ignorance. The citizen who opts out is not just disobedient—they are irresponsible. *This reframing transforms public policy into a moral test.*

Such moral narratives are further reinforced by the convergence of state messaging with platform amplification. Emergency notifications are now pushed through search engines, social media, and mapping services. Partnerships between governments and Big Tech enable real-time nudging, information gating, and visibility throttling. A protest may still occur—but may be quietly delisted from search results or geofenced on maps. A government directive may appear at the top of every app screen, while contradictory views are shadowed or penalised. The content pipeline is curated not just for accuracy, but for alignment. *Truth becomes a matter of platform policy, not civic debate.*

What makes these developments distinct from older models of control is their seamlessness. Traditional authoritarianism relied on force, visible surveillance, and overt restrictions. The contemporary model relies on design, data, and user experience. Behaviour is shaped through interface. Risk is mitigated through automation. Consent is inferred through participation. The less it feels like coercion, the more effective it becomes. *Soft governance achieves what hard power often fails to: it makes obedience feel like virtue.*

Yet beneath the surface lies a serious imbalance of power. The ability to shape norms, distribute access, and define risk increasingly rests with a hybrid ecosystem of state agencies, health authorities, and private technology firms. These actors operate across jurisdictions, often with little transparency or democratic oversight. Their tools are proprietary, their algorithms inaccessible, and their terms of service subject to unilateral change. *This is regulation by infrastructure, not legislation.*

To accept such a model without scrutiny is to invite a future in which policy is less about public deliberation and more about automated enforcement. Health codes become citizen scores. Safety alerts become movement permissions. Inclusion becomes tracking. And every update to the system adds a new layer of dependency. The user has no say in how the platform evolves—they can only accept the terms or be excluded from its benefits. *The citizen is gradually redefined as a data point in a behavioural management system.*

To challenge this trajectory, it is essential to interrogate not just the tools, but the narratives. Why is control always framed as care? Why are citizens asked to trade visibility for access? And why are systems designed with no off switch, no sunset clause, and no civic audit? These are not technical questions—they are political ones. They demand a reinvigoration of public discourse, legal scrutiny, and ethical design.

Benevolent tyranny thrives not because people are powerless, but because the mechanisms of power no longer appear threatening. When surveillance looks like safety, and exclusion feels like protection, resistance becomes socially risky. Yet if liberty is to remain meaningful, it must include the freedom to question what is framed as help. *Not every system built for our benefit is neutral in its effects. And not every act of care is free from the logic of control.*

Compassion as Strategy

One of the most enduring myths in modern governance is that surveillance systems are born out of necessity, not choice. But more often than not, they are born out of opportunity—and justified through language that disarms opposition. Increasingly, humanitarian rhetoric is being used to introduce digital infrastructure that reshapes the relationship between citizen and state. Terms like *inclusion*, *access*, and *empowerment* have become the semantic camouflage for tools of control. And nowhere is this dynamic more visible than in the global rollout of digital ID systems aimed at "serving the poor."

What begins as a promise to extend dignity often ends in increased dependency. A biometric ID card issued to facilitate financial inclusion may later become a precondition for receiving food, schooling, or shelter. A fingerprint enrolled to verify identity may later link to facial recognition databases and predictive risk algorithms. The entry point is compassion; the endpoint is control. *Intent is noble. Outcome is structural.*

Consider India's Aadhaar programme—a biometric identity system introduced as a vehicle to streamline welfare distribution and eliminate corruption. With over 1.3 billion enrollees, it has been widely cited as a model for digital inclusion. Yet its implementation has been marred by exclusions, data breaches, and the erosion of anonymity. In states like Jharkhand, pensioners died after being denied benefits for failure to authenticate their fingerprints. In Rajasthan, ration card holders were turned away from food subsidies because of network failures in the Aadhaar verification system. What was designed to guarantee access inadvertently became a barrier to survival. *The promise of efficiency came at the price of reliability.*

International donors, development banks, and technology vendors often frame these systems as a leap forward—an opportunity to bring the Global South into the digital economy. But they rarely disclose the political bargains embedded in the infrastructure. Who stores the data? Who has access? What happens when the systems fail—or are misused? The framing is always upward: we are giving the poor tools to lift themselves. The reality is often downward: we are enrolling them into opaque systems they cannot opt out of, challenge, or understand.

In Kenya, the Huduma Namba initiative was launched with the stated goal of improving service delivery. Yet it quickly raised alarms among civil liberties groups for its broad scope and lack of safeguards. Citizens were required to provide extensive personal and biometric data, including GPS coordinates of their homes. The system was implemented with limited public debate and no comprehensive data protection legislation in place. Though pitched as inclusive, it effectively created a digital underclass—those without a Huduma Namba found themselves unable to access government services. *Inclusion became exclusion by another name.*

This inversion of meaning is central to understanding how compassion operates as a strategy. It redefines coercion as care. The logic is subtle but pervasive: if you're not in the system, we can't help you. But once you are in, help is conditional. Participation becomes mandatory, benefits discretionary. The individual no longer chooses the terms of engagement—the system does. *Freedom becomes a function of compliance.*

In development discourse, this model is often celebrated under the banner of "leapfrogging." The idea is that poor countries can skip traditional models of infrastructure and adopt digital solutions more quickly. But this also means skipping over the regulatory, legal, and ethical frameworks that took decades to develop elsewhere. Facial recognition in public spaces, algorithmic welfare scoring, predictive policing—these tools are often piloted in communities least equipped to resist them. The developmental logic is seductive: why delay innovation? The ethical trade-offs are seldom discussed.

One example is the collaboration between the World Bank's Identification for Development (ID4D) programme and African governments seeking to digitise their populations. While the initiative rightly identifies gaps in access, it also encourages centralised biometric databases without always guaranteeing constitutional protections. In Ghana, the National Identification Authority launched a mandatory digital ID system linked to healthcare, taxes, and telecom services. Critics warned of "function creep"—where a tool for registration gradually becomes a tool for surveillance. And once linked to financial services, these systems can be used to enforce debt recovery, deny credit, or profile risk. *What began as a humanitarian tool becomes a behavioural instrument.*

A parallel trend can be observed in refugee management. Biometric systems developed under the auspices of humanitarian aid are increasingly being used for surveillance and control. The UNHCR has worked with contractors to collect iris scans and fingerprints from refugees across the Middle East and Africa. Ostensibly, this is to ensure identity and prevent fraud. But the data is often shared with host governments—some of which have a history of persecuting the same populations. Refugees, who by definition lack political power, find themselves locked into systems they neither requested nor consented to. *Aid becomes data extraction.*

What these examples illustrate is not merely a technical issue, but a structural one. The narrative of compassion allows invasive systems to be introduced without public resistance. They are seen not as surveillance tools, but as interventions. The state is not expanding its power—it is simply helping. But if access to help requires biometric verification, if assistance comes with tracking, if support is conditional on compliance, then the distinction between aid and governance collapses. *The politics of care becomes a cover for the politics of control.*

The ethical tension lies in the asymmetry between intent and impact. No one questions the need to improve access to services or prevent corruption. But when the means involve permanent enrolment into centralised databases, algorithmic eligibility scoring, and unaccountable platform partnerships, the risks multiply. These systems are often irreversible. You can't delete your biometric profile. You can't opt out of a programme that governs your ability to eat, move, or survive. The citizen is reduced to a digital artefact—recorded, ranked, and routed by systems they cannot interrogate. *The poor become transparent before they become visible.*

There is also a troubling conflation of trust with documentation. In many of these schemes, the unbanked, undocumented, or stateless are portrayed as problems to be solved through data. But a lack of papers is not always a lack of identity—it is often a reflection of exclusion. Solving that through digitisation risks reinforcing the same power structures under a new guise. When documentation becomes the prerequisite for rights, the undocumented are rendered rightless. *The act of caring must not become the act of capturing.*

This is not a rejection of digital tools, but a demand for clarity, consent, and accountability. Systems must be judged not only by their intent but by their design and governance. Who owns the infrastructure? What legal recourse do individuals have? Can a citizen contest a system-generated denial? These are not secondary questions. They are central to whether digital inclusion strengthens democracy—or hollows it out.

Compassion must not be reduced to a vector for compliance. If the goal is to empower, the systems must be auditable. If the aim is to uplift, the technology must be optional. And if the promise is dignity, the infrastructure must be reversible. Anything less is not inclusion. It is enrolment into a new form of governance—where the price of help is the forfeiture of agency. *And the architecture of care becomes indistinguishable from the architecture of control.*

Welfare or Weapon?

The word *welfare* suggests care, protection, and the fulfilment of basic needs. It evokes images of support in times of hardship, an infrastructure of dignity that levels the playing field when the odds are stacked too high. But increasingly, welfare systems are being redesigned not as lifelines, but as behavioural contracts. And in the process, they are quietly becoming tools of discipline. *The shift is not only administrative—it is philosophical.* What once served to empower now seeks to monitor. What once assumed trust now demands proof.

At the centre of this transformation is conditionality: the idea that assistance must be earned, verified, and continuously revalidated. This is not new. Welfare states have long imposed requirements on recipients. But what has changed is the technological infrastructure—and the scale of enforcement. Today, eligibility is determined not just by income or circumstance, but by algorithms. Cash is not simply delivered; it is tied to biometric IDs, behavioural tracking, and predictive analytics. *The beneficiary becomes a data subject, and the system becomes an instrument of oversight.*

In India, the Mahatma Gandhi National Rural Employment Guarantee Act (MGNREGA)—a flagship rural welfare programme—was integrated with Aadhaar, the country's massive biometric ID system. In principle, this was meant to ensure transparency and prevent fraud. In practice, it introduced new layers of exclusion. Wages were delayed or denied due to authentication errors. Workers were forced to queue at malfunctioning biometric terminals. The very system designed to reduce corruption created new points of failure—technical, bureaucratic, and social. The burden shifted to the individual: prove your identity, prove your presence, prove your poverty. *Assistance became conditional not on need, but on navigability.*

Brazil's Bolsa Família programme, long praised for its impact on poverty reduction, also evolved into a model of conditionality. Families received cash transfers if they met health and education requirements—vaccination schedules, school attendance, prenatal visits. On paper, this was an elegant integration of social goals and financial support. But when scaled and automated, these conditions created pressure points. Miss a health appointment due to a transportation strike? Risk losing your benefit. Fall short of attendance because your child had to work temporarily? The system doesn't ask why. It only logs the breach. *Automation amplifies rigidity—and reduces space for context.*

What makes this development particularly concerning is the embedding of biometric verification into welfare access. The justification is almost always the same: fraud prevention, better targeting, administrative efficiency. But behind these justifications lies a deeper transformation of the state-citizen relationship. Biometric data—iris scans, fingerprints, facial recognition—becomes a prerequisite for accessing entitlements. Without it, the system doesn't see you. And once you're in, your every interaction becomes trackable. In Pakistan, the Benazir Income Support Programme now requires biometric verification at withdrawal points. Numerous reports have emerged of women—often elderly or disabled—being denied benefits due to fingerprint mismatches. The machine doesn't adapt to the human. The human must conform to the machine.

This convergence of welfare and surveillance is not limited to the Global South. In the United Kingdom, the Department for Work and Pensions (DWP) has increasingly deployed automated fraud detection systems, using algorithms to monitor spending patterns, location data, and behavioural anomalies. Individuals have been flagged—and sanctioned—without explanation, based on models they cannot see or contest. The shift is from discretion to prediction. From human judgement to machine-generated suspicion. *The welfare office becomes a site of risk profiling, not solidarity.*

Basic income pilots, long framed as progressive alternatives to conditionality, are also beginning to show signs of behavioural tethering. In Kenya, GiveDirectly's long-term UBI trial offers unconditional transfers—but only within a tightly monitored framework. Participants are tracked through mobile phones, surveys, and digital feedback loops. The data is anonymised, but the structure is extractive. Aid becomes a research asset. Behaviour becomes a metric. And once these models are scaled, the temptation to embed conditions—or automate adjustments—will be hard to resist. The more we can measure, the more we try to optimise. And what begins as *help* slowly becomes *management.*

The ethical stakes rise when these systems are tied to predictive analytics. In the Netherlands, the now-suspended SyRI (System Risk Indication) programme used algorithmic scoring to identify potential welfare fraud. Entire neighbourhoods were flagged as "high risk" based on opaque criteria—immigration status, housing density, employment history. People were investigated not for what they did, but for where they lived and what their profile suggested they might do. After a legal challenge, the courts ruled SyRI violated human rights. But the precedent remains: *governments are willing to trade presumption of innocence for predictive efficiency.*

And here lies the core dilemma. Welfare, at its best, is a recognition of shared vulnerability. It affirms that dignity should not be contingent on productivity, conformity, or biometric registration. But when systems are redesigned around suspicion—when every transaction is a test, every benefit a conditional—then welfare ceases to be a right. It becomes a reward. And rewards can be revoked.

This transformation is not accidental. It reflects a broader ideology of technocratic governance, where social problems are treated as engineering challenges, and citizens as data flows. The goal is not to understand context but to optimise outcomes. And optimisation, by design, favours surveillance. It favours centralised databases, standardised rules, automated enforcement. It favours predictability over autonomy. *The more efficient the system, the less space it has for dissent.*

Governments are not alone in this shift. Technology firms are increasingly central to welfare delivery—designing infrastructure, processing data, managing platforms. Mastercard's partnership with the World Food Programme to distribute aid in refugee camps is one example. Palantir's role in analysing health data for public benefit programmes in the US is another. These partnerships blur the line between public service and private interest. Citizens interact with welfare systems that are co-managed by commercial entities, governed by contracts they never see, and monitored by systems they cannot question. *Digital assistance becomes digital dependence.*

There is also a psychological cost. When welfare is delivered through systems of scrutiny, it erodes trust. Recipients internalise the belief that they are always being watched, always being evaluated. This creates a climate of compliance, not empowerment. People adjust their behaviour—not to flourish, but to avoid triggering red flags. They under-report income. They avoid protesting. They disengage from politics. *Surveillance suppresses not just fraud, but freedom.*

Some defenders argue that these systems reduce leakages, increase efficiency, and ensure fairness. But fairness cannot be reduced to frictionless processing. Fairness requires accountability, transparency, and human discretion. The risk is not just that people will be wrongly denied help. It is that help will be transformed into a system of quiet coercion—a way to enforce norms, reward docility, and manage the margins of society.

The challenge is not to reject technology, but to insist on its subordination to human rights. Welfare systems must serve the individual, not manage them. Biometric registration should be optional, not mandatory. Predictive analytics must be auditable, not proprietary. Conditionality must be proportionate, not punitive. And above all, the dignity of the citizen must be the cornerstone—not a variable to be weighed in a scoring model.

We must ask: who designs these systems? Who profits from their deployment? Who has the right to opt out? These are not technical questions. They are democratic ones. Because if the price of basic subsistence is biometric compliance and algorithmic surveillance, then what is being offered is not welfare. It is obedience. And obedience, under the guise of care, is the oldest form of control. *When aid becomes conditional on visibility, and support becomes a function of surveillance, we are not uplifting the poor—we are managing them.*

The Infantilized Citizen

A citizen is presumed to be capable—of reason, of judgment, of consent. That has long been the baseline of democratic governance: we legislate, vote, protest, and deliberate because we are believed to possess the mental faculties and moral agency to do so. Increasingly, however, this foundational assumption is being replaced with another—more technocratic, more paternalistic, and far more consequential. *Citizens are not to be trusted with freedom; they are to be managed.* Gently, incrementally, and always in the name of their own good.

This is the quiet logic behind the rise of behavioural policy, "nudging" initiatives, and digitally mediated control systems. It is not that citizens are denied autonomy outright. Rather, they are surrounded by subtle constraints, curated choices, and pre-emptive safeguards that erode it in practice. The state does not say "you may not." It says, "you shouldn't," then designs your environment so that you can't. The architecture of governance is being retooled to simulate consent without requiring it.

The most visible example of this shift emerged during the COVID-19 pandemic. Public health messaging in many countries took on a distinctly parental tone—"stay home," "protect others," "follow the rules." These were often necessary measures. But layered beneath them were app-based quarantines, geofenced alerts, and exposure notification tools that made noncompliance nearly impossible. In Singapore, for instance, citizens were encouraged—then required—to use TraceTogether, a digital contact-tracing app. Initially voluntary, its use was later tied to access to workplaces and public spaces. The individual's judgment about risk or privacy was deemed less relevant than the system's collective logic. *You could choose—but only from a pre-approved menu.*

A more structural version of this thinking is embedded in the "nudge units" that have proliferated within governments. Originating from behavioural economics, these teams aim to steer citizens towards better choices—healthier diets, tax compliance, energy conservation—without coercion. But while nudging is marketed as empowerment, it operates on an assumption of cognitive inadequacy. Citizens are viewed as prone to bias, incapable of self-discipline, and easily distracted. *The response is not education or deliberation, but design.* You won't be taught why something matters; you'll be subtly guided to act as if it does.

Consider the shift in digital government services. Interfaces are increasingly gamified, defaulted, and optimised to direct behaviour. Want to opt out of data sharing? The option is buried three screens deep. Want to challenge a parking ticket or welfare decision? The process is labyrinthine by design. At every turn, citizens are expected to comply passively, not engage critically. When technology replaces transparency with convenience, the user is not empowered—they are placated. *The interface becomes the institution.*

The infantilisation of citizens is not simply a design problem—it is a political strategy. In environments of uncertainty or dissent, it becomes a convenient justification for authority. Populations are treated as fragile, prone to misinformation, and incapable of rational judgment. Therefore, speech must be regulated, information curated, and protests managed. This was evident in the European Union's approach to combating disinformation, where content moderation policies increasingly privilege "trusted" sources and suppress unverified claims—not through censorship, but through algorithmic demotion. The public is not banned from reading dissenting views; they are simply shielded from encountering them.

In the economic domain, the logic is equally clear. The growing popularity of conditional cash transfers, automated budgeting apps, and spending "nudges" for welfare recipients reflects a broader belief that the poor cannot be trusted with money. In the United States, some pilot universal basic income programmes load funds onto debit cards that restrict purchases to essential categories. In Australia, the "Indue card" initiative did the same—prohibiting spending on alcohol or gambling. Supporters framed it as protection. Critics saw it as a digital leash. *Either way, the message was unmistakable: we know better than you do.*

The result is a creeping normalisation of low-agency citizenship. One in which participation is replaced by compliance, and judgement is displaced by defaults. This is particularly acute in smart cities, where urban life is increasingly mediated by sensors, platforms, and predictive systems. Traffic flows, energy use, and even pedestrian movement are monitored and optimised—not just for efficiency, but for behaviour modification. Jaywalking becomes a fineable offence caught by facial recognition. Noise complaints trigger automated warnings. Every interaction becomes an input, every deviation a potential liability. *You are not living in a city; you are operating within a system.*

This tendency is not inherently authoritarian. It often originates from well-meaning intentions: to improve public outcomes, reduce harm, or streamline administration. But that is precisely what makes it difficult to resist. Infantilisation is rarely imposed with force. It arrives as a gesture of care. "We're protecting you." "We're simplifying things." "We're making it easier." Yet in this transaction, something essential is lost. The messy, unpredictable, and occasionally inconvenient character of citizenship is replaced with a polished simulation of participation.

To question this trend is not to advocate for chaos or deregulation. It is to insist that adult agency—the capacity to choose, to disagree, to err—is foundational to democratic life. When systems are designed to remove friction, they also remove resistance. And without resistance, there can be no accountability. *Consent without awareness is not consent. Choice without alternatives is not freedom.*

The deeper problem is epistemic. Infantilised governance assumes that knowledge is asymmetrical and trust must flow one way—from citizen to institution, not the reverse. The expert knows best. The algorithm knows better. The system is too complex to question. This posture creates a gap between ruler and ruled—not just in power, but in perceived capacity. The state becomes the parent; the citizen, the dependent.

Yet history offers cautionary tales. In the Soviet Union, central planning presumed the same asymmetry of knowledge. So did colonial governance structures that dismissed local customs in favour of imported technocracy. Today, the digital state risks repeating this error—replacing local judgment with global code, deliberation with dashboard metrics. The result may be more efficient governance, but it is also more fragile. *A society that forgets how to argue, contest, and dissent is a society that forgets how to govern itself.*

If the infantilised citizen is one end of the spectrum, the empowered citizen must be reclaimed at the other. Not as a data point to be nudged, but as a participant to be engaged. This means designing systems that presume capacity, not deficiency. It means building friction back into governance—not as a bug, but as a safeguard. It means treating disagreement as a feature of democracy, not a threat to order. *Most of all, it means trusting people with the burden of their own judgment.*

Technology will not reverse this trend on its own. If anything, it accelerates it. But political culture can resist it. The demand is not to abandon digital tools, but to subordinate them to civic ends. Nudges must be made visible. Defaults must be contestable. Oversight must be intelligible. And participation must be more than a checkbox. Otherwise, we are not being governed—we are being managed. And the management of adults as if they were children, however subtle or well-intentioned, is not democracy. It is condescension at scale.

Chapter 7

The Psychology of Submission

Submission today does not arrive with a barked order or the stomp of boots. It arrives through design, interface, and convenience—often in settings where individuals still appear to be choosing. Yet choice, in many contemporary environments, is not the freedom it once signified. It is increasingly curated, pre-empted, and engineered to guide behaviour within predetermined boundaries. *This is not coercion in its classic form. It is compliance induced through architecture.*

Modern systems of control do not rely solely on force or explicit threats. They operate through what might be called cognitive compliance: the restructuring of individual perception, behaviour, and expectation until active resistance feels unnecessary—or even unintelligible. The mechanisms of this restructuring are subtle but powerful: the framing of options, the psychology of scarcity and fear, the disincentives of exclusion, and the growing appeal of algorithmic delegation. Collectively, they cultivate not just outward conformity, but *inner resignation.*

This chapter explores the psychological infrastructure that enables systems of control to endure—and expand—without constant surveillance or overt suppression. We are not merely regulated by states or platforms; increasingly, we are *acclimated* to regulation, trained into it by our own habits, anxieties, and assumptions. The true power of today's systems lies not in how they command, but in how they condition.

The first section, *The Illusion of Choice*, interrogates how digital platforms, public institutions, and commercial interfaces shape user behaviour through constrained options—giving the appearance of autonomy while guiding users down predictable paths. Whether selecting privacy settings, navigating customer service bots, or choosing between conditional cash transfer schemes, individuals are increasingly offered "freedom" that has already been pre-sculpted. These are choices not of substance, but of sequence and style. The consequence is an erosion of agency that goes unnoticed—because it feels voluntary.

Yet agency is not only constrained through interface; it is corroded by *incentive structures.* In *Fear and FOMO*, we examine how the architecture of exclusion—social, financial, professional—creates powerful incentives to comply with systems that individuals may distrust, dislike, or fail to understand. A vaccine passport may feel invasive, but the fear of being locked out of travel or employment overrides dissent. An AI-managed hiring platform may seem unfair, but job-seekers accept its terms because there is no other way through. Fear, particularly of missing out or falling behind, is one of the most consistent engines of participation. *Coercion has been replaced by pressure—silent, ambient, and unrelenting.*

Over time, these pressures accumulate not just as burdens, but as beliefs. This leads to *Learned Helplessness at Scale*, a concept borrowed from trauma theory and recontextualised for digitally governed life. When individuals are repeatedly placed in situations where choices feel futile, feedback loops are opaque, and outcomes are non-negotiable, they adapt—not by resisting, but by ceasing to try. Resignation replaces revolt. This is especially visible in marginalised communities, where welfare recipients, undocumented workers, or data-rich but rights-poor populations are subjected to algorithmic systems that decide eligibility, risk, or movement—with no meaningful process for appeal. A person who cannot see a path out of the system stops imagining one.

And even where oppression is not systemic or totalising, there is another force at play: the *voluntary surrender of cognitive labour.* The final section, *Cognitive Offloading and the Loss of Will*, explores how individuals increasingly defer to algorithms, apps, and smart systems to make everyday decisions—from navigation to dating, from budgeting to health tracking. This offloading is not merely a convenience. Over time, it subtly atrophies the human faculties that underpin moral and civic judgment. When we outsource choice, we outsource responsibility. And when enough decisions are delegated, we forget what it meant to deliberate.

The danger is not that people become stupid, but that they become passive. Systems that anticipate our desires before we articulate them, or remove friction so effectively that we no longer consider alternatives, breed a form of passivity that is hard to detect and harder to reverse. The loss is not cognitive in the narrow sense—it is existential. *We begin to experience our own lives not as authors, but as users.*

This chapter is not a critique of digital tools per se. Algorithms, behavioural design, and predictive systems all have legitimate applications. But their psychological effects must be examined with far more rigour than they currently are. When the language of empowerment is used to mask the architecture of compliance, when people believe they are choosing even as their choices are being pre-structured, and when consent becomes indistinguishable from submission, the line between democracy and design begins to blur.

What emerges is a citizen who is not forcibly silenced, but gently managed. A user who is not shackled, but shepherded. A society that appears to function through freedom, yet is governed through nudges, defaults, and disincentives so seamlessly integrated that few notice what has been lost. *The point is not that the new systems are dystopian. The point is that they are domesticated—and that is precisely what makes them effective.*

To explore the psychology of submission is to confront the uncomfortable truth that compliance does not always come from fear or weakness. It often comes from fatigue, convenience, and adaptation. Systems of control today do not need to be terrifying. They only need to be efficient. And when they are, they are all the more difficult to question—because their success becomes self-justifying.

This chapter aims to trace the contours of that success—and its costs. Not to moralise, but to sharpen the reader's awareness. To understand what is happening not only around us, but within us. Because the most potent systems of control are not those that monitor our actions, but those that reshape our expectations. And the most urgent question is not whether we are being ruled, but *how we have come to accept it.*

The Illusion of Choice

Choice has long been positioned as the cornerstone of autonomy. In democratic societies, the act of choosing—between products, services, policies, or lifestyles—is presumed to be both empowering and indicative of personal freedom. But not all choices are equal, and not all freedom is authentic. Increasingly, what is offered as choice is, in fact, choreography: a performance of autonomy within the boundaries of pre-configured options. The menu may appear diverse, but the meal has already been prepared.

Modern interfaces—whether public services, social platforms, or commercial ecosystems—do not restrict decision-making through force. They achieve the same result through structure. By controlling what is visible, available, and frictionless, designers and institutions limit the field of action while allowing users to feel that they are deciding. This is not a hypothetical concern; it is the operational logic behind platforms that shape behaviour not through enforcement, but through engineered experience.

Take the example of a popular ride-hailing app. The user is presented with three options: Standard, Premium, and Shared. Each has a price, an expected wait time, and a level of comfort. This seems like genuine choice, until one notices what's missing. There's no negotiation, no access to alternatives outside the platform, no visibility into how pricing was determined. The algorithm is opaque, the conditions are non-negotiable, and the user has little recourse. The illusion is maintained by the presence of options—but *every* option sustains the system's logic.

This dynamic extends far beyond transportation. In healthcare, digital triage systems now determine which patients see doctors and which are redirected. Algorithms decide eligibility for loans, housing, and welfare—not through public deliberation, but through private scoring models. Crucially, these systems present themselves as offering choice: "Would you like to reschedule?", "Would you prefer this appointment slot?", "Would you like a notification instead of a call?" Yet at the core, the most consequential parameters—*who gets access, under what criteria, and who oversees the decision*—are fixed and concealed.

Public policy has not been immune. Governments increasingly use digital platforms to deliver services, while simultaneously reducing human discretion. A benefits applicant may be asked to choose between different payment plans or submit additional documentation through an online portal. On the surface, this looks like empowerment. But if the platform denies their eligibility and there's no clear path to appeal or human oversight, then choice becomes cosmetic. *The act of choosing is decoupled from influence.*

In retail, the illusion of choice is monetised with ruthless efficiency. Platforms such as Amazon or Google Shopping present users with "recommendations" derived from behavioural profiles. While thousands of products may be technically available, only a curated few are made visible—based on what will likely convert. The user can scroll endlessly, but they are still inside a box shaped by relevance algorithms. There is little difference between an ad that tells you what to buy and a ranking system that only shows what you're likely to want. *One shouts, the other whispers—but both speak for you.*

In political life, this principle takes on even more serious consequences. Electoral systems, ostensibly the most sacred domains of choice, often constrain voters to two or three viable candidates—each representing variations on a narrow ideological spectrum. Voter suppression, media manipulation, and data-driven microtargeting further constrain what voters know, think, and believe is possible. When public opinion is shaped by filtered feeds, targeted misinformation, and algorithmically ranked narratives, the choices available on the ballot begin to resemble the layout of a dropdown menu, not a genuine expression of democratic diversity.

Critically, this isn't just about manipulation. The more insidious effect is *internalisation*. When constrained choices are presented frequently enough, individuals begin to accept the structure as natural. They stop looking for alternatives, not because they agree with the status quo, but because they cannot easily imagine something beyond it. This is where engineered environments shift from being limiting to being formative—they don't just shape behaviour; they shape belief.

Consider the example of digital ID systems that require biometric registration for access to social services. A citizen may be given a choice: register and receive aid, or opt out and be excluded. The presence of a choice here is technical, not meaningful. There is no negotiation, no alternative system, and often no institutional accountability. And yet, to external observers, the programme will be described as "voluntary". The framing of choice is used to sanitise coercion.

There are those who argue that constraints are inevitable, and to some degree they are correct. No system can offer unlimited options without collapsing into chaos. However, the issue is not the presence of constraints, but their *concealment*. When limits are imposed transparently—when users understand the trade-offs and the logic behind them—choice remains informed. But when constraints are hidden behind slick interfaces, algorithmic logic, or bureaucratic opacity, then choice becomes a ritual: a gesture toward agency, not its practice.

This is particularly troubling in the context of children's and teenagers' interactions with digital platforms. Personalisation engines in educational tools, content platforms, and even virtual learning environments present structured decisions—"choose your learning path", "select your interests"—that simulate agency while locking young users into developmental channels designed by others. The long-term impact is still unfolding, but early studies suggest that habituation to structured choice may reduce creative problem-solving and increase dependence on external feedback loops.

From a governance standpoint, the use of structured choice has become an administrative shortcut. Why design complex policies with deliberative flexibility when you can outsource decision-making to digital systems that streamline compliance? Why build trust when you can manufacture assent through UX? The ethical risk here is not just authoritarian creep. It's the *unconscious abandonment of democratic complexity* in favour of managerial simplicity.

At a cultural level, the repeated exposure to constrained choice rewires public expectations. Citizens begin to ask for better interfaces instead of better rights. They seek more "user-friendly" forms of control, rather than asking who designs the controls in the first place. Political language adapts accordingly: governments describe surveillance policies as "opt-in security" and data harvesting as "personalised service". When resistance is framed as inefficiency and submission as convenience, the architecture of freedom quietly collapses.

There are ways forward—but they begin with awareness. Recognising the difference between real choice and its simulation is not merely a cognitive exercise. It is a civic imperative. Systems that offer pre-approved options while denying structural influence must be confronted, not accepted as inevitable. Regulatory bodies need to require algorithmic transparency, especially when public services are being delegated to private infrastructures. Education systems must teach not just digital literacy, but *design literacy*—an understanding of how environments shape perception and preference.

More broadly, there needs to be a reassertion of public imagination. To reclaim the idea of choice is to expand the set of what can be chosen—not just between pre-set options, but between models, systems, and values. This does not mean romanticising total freedom; it means resisting the quiet standardisation of everything. When freedom is redefined as the ability to pick from a limited set of outcomes, designed by someone else, for purposes you cannot inspect, then the project of autonomy is not only weakened—it is domesticated.

And yet, the act of seeing is itself a beginning. When the structure becomes visible, the possibility of resistance returns. The first step is not rebellion. It is recognition. And from recognition comes redefinition—not just of what we choose, but of how, and why, and with what level of consent. That is where autonomy lives. Not in the number of choices, but in the scope of our influence over them.

Fear and FOMO

No coercive system succeeds without consent—but not all consent is freely given. Increasingly, people don't opt into digital infrastructures because they trust them, believe in them, or even fully understand them. They comply because they fear the cost of exclusion. In a world where access to services, work, healthcare, and even identity itself is being tied to digital credentials and behavioural conformity, saying no can mean opting out of modern life altogether. And so, people say yes. Not with enthusiasm, but with anxiety. Not because they want to, but because they feel they must.

This is how *fear* has become a functional operating system for digital governance.

Consider the rapid global adoption of biometric ID systems. In countries like India, Kenya, and Nigeria, these programmes are promoted as breakthroughs in inclusion. Yet for millions of individuals, registration is not a choice but a precondition: no ID, no pension. No ID, no school. No ID, no food subsidy. The decision to participate is often framed as voluntary, but the consequences of opting out are so severe that participation becomes inevitable. This isn't inclusion. It's conditionality masquerading as empowerment.

At the heart of this coercion is a social contract rewritten in silence. The traditional idea of a contract assumes mutual understanding and agency. But when people are nudged, pressured, or economically cornered into adopting surveillance-laced technologies, the result is not consent—it is capitulation. What changes is not only *what* people are required to do, but the terms on which their agency is defined. The power dynamic shifts subtly but decisively from negotiation to compliance.

The pandemic accelerated this shift. The deployment of vaccine passports, digital contact tracing, and mobility apps introduced a new normal: prove your compliance or lose access. While many of these tools were introduced under the banner of public health, their design mirrored enforcement architectures rather than care infrastructures. In countries such as France and Israel, access to cafes, workplaces, and even public transportation was tied to digital proof of vaccination. While the public debates focused on health efficacy, the deeper shift was procedural—introducing new norms of behavioural certification that normalised exclusion as a legitimate administrative tool.

For most people, the fear was not ideological. It was practical. Miss your compliance window, and you can't enter your university. Lose your phone, and you're barred from the job site. Ask too many questions, and you risk bureaucratic retaliation. The trade-offs weren't theoretical—they played out in wages, routines, and reputations. This is how compliance culture embeds itself: through exhaustion, not enthusiasm. The path of least resistance becomes the only viable one.

Parallel mechanisms can be seen in the workplace. Increasingly, employers require prospective hires to submit to AI-driven assessments that profile their voice, facial expressions, or keystroke patterns. These tools claim to detect soft skills or predict job fit, but the reality is far murkier. The assessments are opaque, their scientific grounding often dubious, and their outcomes unchallengeable. Yet candidates comply—not because they trust the process, but because *not* participating means being filtered out. The choice is illusory: submit or disappear from consideration.

This dynamic is even more pronounced in the platform economy. Take rideshare drivers in California or warehouse workers in the UK. Algorithmic management systems monitor their every move, from speed and delivery times to tone of customer interaction. Deviation from optimised behaviour—even for valid reasons like rest or safety—can result in deactivation. Workers are given dashboards to track performance and "improve," but these tools do not provide genuine agency. They function more like behavioural mirrors, rewarding those who conform and quietly removing those who don't. The result is a culture of hypervigilance, where fear of disconnection drives total self-monitoring.

The psychological term for this is *functional compliance*—when people adhere to a system not out of belief but to avoid penalties. But digital systems have refined this into a subtler form: compliance by FOMO—*fear of missing out*. In professional networks, not being on LinkedIn or industry platforms can mean invisibility. In dating, not joining the dominant app ecosystem effectively erases one's presence. In finance, those without digital credit scores are rendered unbanked. Participation becomes self-reinforcing, even when trust is eroding, because the perceived cost of opting out always exceeds the known risk of staying in.

This is how systems grow powerful: not because people love them, but because people fear being left behind.

Importantly, this isn't always driven by authoritarian states. In many cases, liberal democracies and private firms are the ones deploying exclusionary architectures. The European Union's recent push for the Digital Identity Wallet—a system meant to unify credentials across member states—has sparked debate not because it is malicious, but because it introduces dependencies. If public transport, medical access, university registration, and tax filings are all tethered to a single wallet, then the stakes of "opting out" become existential. Participation becomes less about preference and more about eligibility for life itself.

In Iran and Myanmar, by contrast, digital exclusion has taken more violent forms. In the wake of protests, regimes in both countries have used digital ID systems and mobile metadata to isolate dissidents from essential services. If your SIM card is registered to your identity, and that identity is flagged, then you may find your bank account frozen, your internet cut off, or your movement restricted. This is not surveillance in theory—it is administrative erasure.

These extreme examples might seem distant from Western democracies, but the underlying logic is spreading. Increasingly, governments and corporations do not need to persuade—they only need to configure systems such that opting out is intolerable. And once enough people are inside the system, social norms shift. The one who resists becomes the deviant. The sceptic becomes the problem. *Trust is no longer required. All that matters is compliance.*

Yet there is an important distinction to be made between fear and coercion. Coercion is explicit: do this or face punishment. Fear, by contrast, is ambient. It works through anticipation—of losing convenience, opportunity, or connection. And this makes it harder to confront, because it is embedded not in edicts, but in design. It hides in user agreements, app defaults, and workflow requirements. It speaks in the language of user experience, not authoritarian decree.

The challenge, then, is epistemic. How do we name a system that never formally threatens us, but constantly manipulates our fears? How do we critique structures that do not break laws, but silently reshape the terms of participation? The answer begins with recognising that fear-based compliance is not an anomaly—it is an emerging model of governance. A model where power does not enforce but entices, not with freedom but with fear of its absence.

This has profound implications for how resistance is imagined. Traditional civil disobedience relies on visibility: mass protests, public refusals, legal challenges. But in a system where exclusion is algorithmic and opt-out means self-deprivation, resistance becomes internalised and fragmented. People may resent the systems they use but lack the energy, tools, or community to challenge them. This is not apathy. It is fatigue. A fatigue engineered by systems that reward silence and punish friction.

To reverse this trajectory, responses must be equally systemic. Regulatory frameworks must not only target overt abuses but examine how fear-based incentives are built into everyday infrastructures. Data protection laws must address *design coercion*—the practice of structuring systems so that users feel compelled to share or comply. Public institutions must resist outsourcing essential services to platforms that monetise participation. And civil society must cultivate alternatives—systems that *do not punish disconnection.*

Ultimately, the most dangerous systems are not the ones that say "no freedom for you." They are the ones that say, "Here's your freedom—just scan, click, and accept." When fear becomes the price of participation, and FOMO the engine of consent, then the line between autonomy and acquiescence begins to blur. The task now is to redraw that line—clearly, deliberately, and with the understanding that real freedom cannot be conditional on constant submission.

Learned Helplessness at Scale

At a certain point, people stop resisting. Not because they believe the system is right, or just, or even tolerable—but because they've concluded it cannot be changed. This state of resignation, where challenge feels pointless and protest feels futile, is not merely a psychological response. It is a political condition. And it is being engineered—quietly, systematically, and at scale.

In the 1960s, psychologist Martin Seligman introduced the concept of *learned helplessness* to describe what happens when individuals are repeatedly subjected to stressors they cannot control or escape. Over time, they internalise the futility of resistance, ceasing even to try. What began as a study in animal psychology has, disturbingly, found renewed relevance in the digital age—not just in individuals but across entire societies, where algorithmic governance and technological saturation have created environments where power is distributed but accountability is absent.

In a digitally saturated environment, the average person is bombarded by systems that affect their opportunities, visibility, and autonomy—without any meaningful way to interrogate or influence them. Credit scoring algorithms silently approve or deny loans. Recommendation systems determine which jobs are seen, which voices are amplified, and which users are shadow-banned. Smart city sensors, health-tracking apps, behaviour-scoring platforms, biometric logins—each interface promises efficiency, safety, convenience. But they also entrench asymmetries of power that cannot be negotiated by the individual.

It is not just the surveillance itself that induces helplessness. It is the sheer opacity. When decisions are made by systems you cannot see, governed by rules you do not know, and enforced through interfaces you cannot question, resistance begins to feel not only risky but pointless. And over time, people adjust. They withdraw, comply, minimise exposure. They learn to self-censor. They give up on appealing decisions that appear arbitrary, or on challenging platforms that never respond. *Disempowerment becomes a lifestyle.*

This process is not dramatic. It is incremental, quiet, and routinised. Consider how most users interact with online terms of service. They do not read them. They click "agree" not because they are comfortable but because they have learned it is the only viable path forward. Consider the average social media user who, after being wrongly flagged or restricted, simply starts a new account rather than trying to challenge the system. Or the jobseeker who tailors their CV to keyword-optimising software rather than human readers. These are not signs of engagement—they are signals of exhaustion.

The effects of this ambient defeatism are particularly visible in marginalised communities. In India, millions of citizens have been locked out of welfare entitlements due to mismatches between their Aadhaar biometric profiles and government databases. Many of them do not protest. They simply accept the denial of rations or pensions as an error they cannot fix. In the US, tenants in algorithmically-managed buildings report that facial recognition systems fail to recognise them—but they don't complain, fearing eviction or being labelled a security risk. In Kenya, where digital ID is now tied to essential services, communities that were historically excluded from registration simply stop trying to appeal. They have internalised the message: the system is final. *Your struggle will not change it.*

What we are witnessing is not just technical failure. It is a broader erosion of political imagination. People cease to believe that systems can be made accountable, that rules can be rewritten, or that participation can shape outcomes. The very notion of "rights" becomes abstract when every grievance is met with silence, automation, or deflection. The interface replaces the institution. And with that shift, protest becomes unthinkable—not because it is illegal, but because it feels irrelevant.

This passivity is often mistaken for consent. Governments and corporations interpret the absence of protest as approval. But that reading is dangerously naïve. What looks like quiet satisfaction is, in many cases, silent resignation. People are not happy with surveillance. They are fatigued by its inevitability. They are not excited about behavioural tracking. They are too tired to resist another policy rollout that will happen with or without their input. *The cost of caring begins to outweigh the perceived benefit of engagement.*

Design plays a critical role in shaping this helplessness. Most digital systems are not built to be challenged. They are optimised for compliance, not negotiation. There is no space to ask "why" an algorithm behaved the way it did. There is no phone number to call when facial recognition fails. There is no recourse when a machine learning model predicts you're too risky to insure, too likely to default, or too controversial to promote. And when channels of redress are systematically absent, people adjust their expectations downward. They stop hoping for fairness. They start strategising around the inevitability of harm.

Children in controlled environments often develop adaptive behaviours to avoid punishment—staying quiet, staying small, not asking questions. Increasingly, adults in digital systems do the same. Not because they are naïve, but because they are rational. It makes sense to limit self-expression when your social score is on the line. It is safer to say nothing when your employer monitors keystrokes or your housing depends on behavioural metrics. *Helplessness, in these contexts, is not irrational—it is survival.*

Yet this state of learned helplessness is politically dangerous. A democracy relies on citizens who believe they can influence systems. A society governed by invisible code and automated rulings risks replacing deliberation with fatalism. The cost is not just personal—it is collective. When too many people give up on the idea of justice as achievable, governance becomes a one-way transaction: data flows up, power flows down, and dissent disappears into silence.

Some may argue that digital systems are neutral, that users should adapt, and that minor errors are inevitable in large-scale automation. But this misses the point. The issue is not occasional technical malfunction—it is the consistent absence of transparency, accountability, and human repair. Systems that cannot be questioned produce populations that no longer try to ask. This is not consent. It is quiet surrender.

To break this cycle, systems must be reimagined to cultivate agency, not just compliance. Interfaces must explain decisions, not just execute them. Appeals must be accessible, not performative. And citizens must be treated not as data subjects, but as political actors with rights, voice, and capacity for refusal. Anything less entrenches the problem it claims to solve.

We should not be asking whether people are using a system. We should be asking whether they feel they *can* challenge it. Whether they understand it. Whether they believe it listens. And when they don't—when the dominant affect becomes numbness, withdrawal, or passive adaptation—we should recognise that as a crisis, not an endorsement.

Learned helplessness is not a bug in digital society. It is a feature of systems that assume scale matters more than legitimacy, that efficiency matters more than fairness, and that quiet users are satisfied ones. But silence does not mean peace. Often, it means exhaustion. And if democracy is to survive the digital transition, we must insist on systems that invite challenge, not produce submission.

Cognitive Offloading and the Loss of Will

A system that remembers for us, recommends for us, decides for us, and increasingly *acts* for us is not just serving us—it is gradually replacing us. In the name of convenience, precision, and optimisation, algorithmic systems have begun to assume the role once held by deliberate human judgment. What began as a functional shortcut—setting a reminder, using GPS, filtering email—has evolved into a structural shift in agency. When we delegate too much, we stop deciding. And when we stop deciding, we begin to forget how.

Cognitive offloading refers to the process of shifting mental tasks to external systems. It is not a new behaviour. Humans have always relied on tools to extend memory and judgement—from notepads and maps to schedules and calculators. But what marks the current era is not just the scale or speed of offloading—it is *who* we offload to, and *what* we lose in the process. Unlike traditional tools that extend cognition, many digital systems do not just support decision-making; they replace it. They filter, nudge, rank, predict, and automate—often invisibly—while users passively adapt to their logics.

Consider the act of choosing what to read, watch, or listen to. Streaming services offer personalised recommendations based on previous behaviour, aggregated trends, and engagement metrics. Users follow these suggestions not because they trust the algorithm's intent, but because the effort of choosing has become too costly. The same holds true for newsfeeds optimised for virality, or navigation apps that determine the "best" route without explaining the trade-offs. *Convenience is not neutral. It carries a cognitive and ethical cost.*

The long-term implications of this automation go beyond preferences.

They touch the core of what it means to exercise agency. When users allow recommendation systems to dictate choices in finance, health, education, relationships, and even parenting, they increasingly orient their behaviour around *what the system expects.* This is not passive support—it is behavioural scripting. The system remembers not just *for* you, but *instead* of you. And over time, that difference becomes irreversible.

This trend is most visible in contexts of moral or social complexity. In medical triage platforms, predictive algorithms propose treatment pathways based on population-level data. In criminal justice systems, software predicts recidivism risk to inform bail or sentencing decisions. In hiring, personality scores and psychometric data guide the filtering of candidates. In these examples, humans remain "in the loop"—but often only nominally. Decision-makers defer to algorithmic outputs because they appear objective, data-backed, and efficient. But this deference erodes scrutiny. *The tool becomes a shield, the system becomes the authority.*

What gets lost in this shift is not just individual decision-making but moral responsibility. When an algorithm suggests the next action, the human is absolved of reflection. "It's what the system recommended" becomes a rationalisation for inaction, exclusion, or error. Over time, people begin to treat recommendation not as suggestion but as mandate. And once moral responsibility is outsourced, the capacity for ethical reasoning begins to decay. What is rewarded is not discernment, but compliance.

At the societal level, the cumulative effect of this offloading is a narrowing of will. People increasingly defer to systems they do not understand, in contexts they do not control, to make decisions they will not question. *Agency is not lost through force. It is surrendered through habit.* The system does not ask for your will; it asks for your data. And in exchange, it offers a frictionless path through increasingly complex terrains. The reward is ease. The cost is authorship.

This dynamic is particularly insidious in environments designed to reduce friction. Digital interfaces are built for instant response: tap, swipe, click, scroll. The more seamless the interaction, the less space there is for deliberation. The architecture of decision-making is compressed into default options, optimised flows, and machine learning predictions. Users follow prompts not because they are coerced, but because they are tired, rushed, or unsure. *Ease displaces reflection, and reflection becomes a burden.*

Even education, once a domain grounded in critical engagement, is being transformed by automated tutoring, behaviour-monitoring dashboards, and AI-generated content recommendations. The student no longer chooses what to study based on curiosity or challenge, but on what the system flags as optimal. Similarly, in health, wearable technologies interpret body data and suggest actions, often reducing complex physiological processes to coloured rings or nudges. Over time, users stop listening to their bodies and begin listening to the device. *Self-knowledge becomes device knowledge.*

This cognitive atrophy has implications not just for individual development but for democratic society. A citizenry habituated to delegation will not easily reclaim agency. Public discourse becomes vulnerable to manipulation when individuals rely on platforms to curate information. Civic engagement weakens when decisions are seen as too complex or too optimised to question. The line between user and subject begins to blur. And when most choices are made elsewhere, *the very meaning of participation is reduced to interaction with a screen.*

There are counterarguments, of course. Some argue that automation liberates attention for higher-order thinking. That by offloading routine or data-intensive decisions, humans are free to focus on values, strategy, or creativity. This is theoretically sound—but it assumes the systems we rely on are designed to preserve that higher-order engagement. Many are not. Most are engineered to maximise retention, predictability, and passive compliance. *Optimisation is not the same as empowerment.* And when the system is opaque, the space for reflection disappears, not expands.

To recover will, systems must be redesigned not just for accuracy or speed, but for *meaningful engagement.* Friction should be built in where the stakes are high. Users must be given insight into why a recommendation was made, what assumptions underlie it, and what alternatives exist. More importantly, they must retain the option to override it. The presence of a human in the loop means little if that human has no room—or habit—of exercising judgment.

Ultimately, the danger is not that machines will think for us. It is that we will forget how to think for ourselves. That we will conflate automation with wisdom, prediction with truth, and suggestion with instruction. *When the cost of effort outweighs the habit of reflection, the will erodes.* And once gone, it is not easily restored.

Cognitive offloading is not inherently dangerous. But when it becomes unthinking, uncritical, and unreciprocated, it ceases to serve us and begins to shape us. The mind, like a muscle, requires resistance to stay strong. A life navigated entirely through optimised choices is not a life lived with agency.

It is a life scripted by systems that are built to predict, not to understand.

The challenge ahead is not to resist technology—but to insist on systems that sharpen, rather than dull, the human capacity for judgment. Systems that amplify our will, rather than render it obsolete. Systems that ask us not just what we want, but why—and leave enough space for us to answer.

Chapter 8

Resistance by Design

The apparatus of control is often assumed to be monolithic—state-sanctioned, corporately maintained, and technologically infallible. Yet systems, no matter how tightly engineered, are never absolute. They are vulnerable not only to malfunction but to subversion. Every infrastructure of surveillance carries within it the potential for refusal. Every mechanism of digital dominance is shadowed by a margin of resistance. And increasingly, that resistance is deliberate, intelligent, and strategic. This chapter examines the growing field of *resistance by design*: not merely opposition to technological control, but the creative reconfiguration of its very foundations.

Control systems are not only technical artefacts; they are moral architectures. They shape possibilities, constrain behaviours, and channel populations into predictable flows. But what happens when those flows are redirected from within? What if the tools of the system—its codebases, protocols, and platforms—are not merely objects of critique, but materials for counter-design? Across the world, designers, civic technologists, whistleblowers, and grassroots movements are engaging in this reimagining. Not by stepping outside the system, but by reaching into it, rearranging its logic, and exposing its fractures.

Consider the act of whistleblowing—not as a lone defiance, but as a structural intervention. From Edward Snowden's revelations about global surveillance to Frances Haugen's disclosures about algorithmic harm at Facebook, these are not simply leaks. They are acts of *design interruption*. They rupture the smooth functioning of opaque systems by injecting public accountability. Similarly, civic technologists in Taiwan, Kenya, and Brazil are coding public-interest platforms that make invisible bureaucracies legible, transform closed data into civic tools, and redesign participation itself. They are not asking for permission. They are creating alternatives.

Resistance also takes material form. In an age of biometric identity, cashless commerce, and digital-only service provision, the preservation of *analogue sanctuaries* has become a radical act. Communities that insist on cash, paper documentation, face-to-face governance, or offline rituals are not simply nostalgic. They are resisting forced digitisation. Indigenous activists maintaining oral data sovereignty; elders refusing mobile health tracking; parents protesting facial recognition in schools—each is asserting the value of unquantified, unmonetised, *unmapped* life. To insist on non-digital options today is not regression. It is design pluralism.

But subversion is not always oppositional. Some forms of resistance come camouflaged within compliance. Counter-design can take the form of spoofing, obfuscation, or gaming the system. Apps like *Face Dazzle* scramble facial recognition. Browser plug-ins flood trackers with fake data. Disinformation detection tools reverse engineer the operations of propaganda bots. These are not merely technological curiosities. They are *tactical responses* to an environment in which citizens are tracked, classified, and scored by default. In such contexts, deception becomes a form of truth-telling. Manipulating the system is not about undermining it irrationally—it is about *exposing its assumptions* and reclaiming space for ambiguity, dissent, and unpredictability.

There is, however, a deeper ethical terrain to navigate. Not all obstruction is virtuous. Not all sabotage is just. The line between resistance and harm is thin, especially when intentions are opaque and tools are universal. When, for instance, is it ethical to mislead a surveillance system? Does an activist's moral right to hide from unjust data collection extend to falsifying documents or identities? Should civic technologists build spoofing tools that could also be exploited by bad actors? The ethics of obstruction demand more than good intentions. They require clarity about context, power, and proportionality. Resistance, to retain its integrity, must be ethically grounded—even when it is tactically subversive.

This chapter is not about nostalgia for the pre-digital past, nor is it an uncritical celebration of all acts that challenge authority. Rather, it is a serious inquiry into *design as political agency*. Technology does not only constrain; it can be reimagined. Systems are not destiny. They are propositions. And every proposition can be re-written.

Readers will encounter examples of designers embedding friction into interfaces to slow down automated decision-making. Of activists building parallel structures to challenge state-run identity systems. Of communities who deliberately limit their digital footprint, not out of fear, but out of conviction. You will see how anonymity, slowness, decentralisation, and ambiguity—once seen as limitations—are now emerging as strategic design principles in a world addicted to speed, clarity, and centralisation.

Yet perhaps the most important insight of this chapter is that resistance by design is not simply about tools. It is about imagination. It is about who gets to define what counts as "secure," "efficient," or "rational." It is about asking whose interests are served by seamlessness, whose values are embedded in protocols, and whose futures are being excluded by current systems. It is about designing not just against domination—but for dignity.

The reader will come away with a deeper understanding of the creative, ethical, and political dimensions of resistance in a digitised world. Not resistance as reaction, but as proposition. Not just refusal, but *redesign*. This chapter invites you to think critically about what counts as participation, autonomy, and agency when technology becomes ambient, and compliance becomes default. It does not offer easy answers. But it insists that *answers must be designed*, and that *design is never neutral.*

Ultimately, this chapter asks: What does it mean to resist *well*? Not in the romantic sense of defiance, but in the disciplined sense of integrity. How do we build systems that honour dissent without collapsing into chaos? How do we code for ambiguity, legislate for resistance, and engineer for refusal—without surrendering to cynicism? To explore these questions is not only to reclaim design as a site of political struggle. It is to insist that the future is still open. And that the blueprint of control, however elaborate, can always be rewritten.

Subverting the System from Within

Most systems of control don't collapse from external pressure—they are destabilised from the inside. The most effective challenges to technocratic power rarely begin with protest banners or barricades. They often start with a line of code, a leaked document, or a quietly subversive design decision. In a world where power is increasingly embedded in infrastructure, resistance is evolving—not through dramatic revolution, but through disciplined, intentional acts of reconfiguration from within. This article explores how whistleblowers, designers, and civic technologists are not merely pushing back against digital control systems but are strategically repurposing them to expose, disrupt, and reimagine power.

The defining feature of modern governance is not its brutality, but its sophistication. Systems of surveillance and algorithmic decision-making are designed not only to monitor but to persuade, nudge, and normalise. They function through complexity and opacity, often shielded by technical jargon, intellectual authority, and corporate confidentiality. In such an environment, the question becomes not merely how to resist—but *where* resistance can take root. Increasingly, the most incisive answers come from individuals who have direct access to these systems, who understand their architecture, and who choose to challenge them at the level of logic and protocol.

Edward Snowden's disclosures in 2013 shifted the public's understanding of state surveillance in a way no campaign or advocacy effort had managed. It wasn't just that the information was shocking—it was that the details came from within the system itself. Snowden didn't act out of ignorance of the risks; he acted from informed conviction, understanding both the machinery of surveillance and the legal shields protecting it. His intervention reframed mass data collection from a security measure to a political choice. It also marked a strategic turn in whistleblowing: not as reactive protest, but as systemic literacy repurposed for accountability.

Frances Haugen's release of internal Facebook documents in 2021 followed a similar arc. Her testimony showed that the harms caused by Facebook's algorithmic amplification—especially to young users' mental health—were not unknown or accidental. They were documented, discussed, and ultimately deprioritised in favour of engagement metrics. Haugen didn't just leak files. She translated the company's internal language into a public reckoning. Like Snowden, she acted not in rejection of technology, but out of an ethical commitment to its responsible use.

Yet whistleblowing is only one mode of subversion. Designers and civic technologists are exploring a broader strategy: to challenge power not by tearing down systems, but by redesigning them. In Kenya, for example, civic developers built *Mzalendo*, a platform that tracks the performance of Members of Parliament. It scrapes parliamentary records, voting data, and attendance logs, converting opaque institutional data into readable civic information. In Brazil, *Operação Serenata de Amor* uses AI to analyse government expenses and identify irregularities in public spending. The system tweets anomalies automatically, holding politicians accountable through algorithmic transparency. These aren't apps for entertainment. They're *counter-infrastructures*, built with the same digital logic as the systems they critique.

In Taiwan, civic hacker collective *g0v* (pronounced "gov-zero") exemplifies what it means to subvert governance through design. Their approach is not antagonistic but complementary. They build open-source versions of government websites and services, improving usability, transparency, and public participation. When Taiwan's digital minister Audrey Tang emerged from this community, it symbolised a radical shift: technologists entering government not to perpetuate opacity but to *refactor it*—to rebuild public institutions with civic accountability coded in.

These examples signal a broader design principle: that resistance can be infrastructural. Rather than attacking institutions from the outside, it is possible to enter the design logic of those institutions and modify their operations. This requires not only technical skill but moral clarity and institutional fluency. It also requires patience. Unlike disruptive protests or viral campaigns, infrastructural resistance is slow, meticulous, and often invisible. But its impact is lasting. It doesn't just expose problems—it changes what is possible within the system.

However, the ethical terrain of internal resistance is complex. When does subversion become sabotage? Can an employee's act of conscience undermine broader organisational goals? Are whistleblowers always morally justified, or do they carry their own biases and agendas? And when civic technologists build tools that interface with public data, how do they balance innovation with responsibility, especially in politically volatile environments? These are not hypothetical questions—they are active tensions. Subversion is not always noble. But when grounded in transparency and directed toward public interest, it becomes a form of democratic repair.

There is also a broader conceptual shift taking place. Traditional models of resistance framed power as something external to be resisted. But in digital systems, power is *ambient*. It is embedded in infrastructure, interfaces, and workflows. To subvert it requires more than opposition—it requires literacy in how systems *function*. Civic technologists must understand databases, application programming interfaces (APIs), and data models—not to glorify them, but to recognise where leverage exists. In a sense, resistance today demands *systems thinking as a moral stance*.

Moreover, acts of internal subversion often blur the boundary between legality and legitimacy. Many civic hacks operate in legal grey zones: scraping public data that is technically open but administratively inaccessible; reverse-engineering APIs that were never meant for public use; or mapping government workflows that agencies prefer to obscure. These tactics are not criminal in intent, but they do challenge bureaucratic control over information. The question is not whether these actions are legal, but whether they serve the public's right to understand—and redesign—the systems that govern them.

Subversion also takes collective form. The civic technology movement is increasingly global, decentralised, and networked. Code written in Argentina is adapted in Nigeria. Transparency tools developed in the Philippines are deployed in Ukraine. Design patterns are shared, forked, and remixed across borders. What emerges is a form of *transnational resistance*, not grounded in ideology, but in open protocols and shared values. In these communities, the idea of government-as-platform is reclaimed—not as a vector of control, but as a space for collaborative redesign.

At the same time, technologists must confront the risk of co-option. Open-source tools are easily appropriated. Civic platforms can be bought out or absorbed by the same institutions they seek to reform. The act of subverting from within carries the danger of assimilation. Resisting this requires not only technical independence but sustained community governance and ethical clarity. Internal resistance is not a single act—it is a long-term commitment to redesign without capture.

The reader should not mistake this for utopianism. Most of the actors profiled here are not idealists. They are pragmatists who understand that systemic change is slow, that failures are inevitable, and that progress often means choosing the least-worst option. But they also understand that in the absence of resistance, systems calcify. They become impervious to reform. They drift from public service toward institutional self-preservation. Subversion, then, is not a rejection of systems. It is an insistence that systems must serve *people*, not merely processes.

This article has focused on individuals and communities who, rather than withdraw or revolt, have chosen to *intervene*. Their work is slow, technical, and often thankless. Yet it is indispensable. Because in an age when power is administered by code, mediated by platforms, and enforced by algorithms, the tools of liberation must speak the language of control systems—not to reinforce them, but to repurpose them. Subverting from within is not the only path. But it is among the most effective, most precise, and most enduring. It is the resistance that knows the wiring.

Analog Sanctuaries

In a world increasingly driven by digital traceability, the act of choosing not to be seen—economically, bureaucratically, or behaviourally—has become both radical and urgent. Analog systems, once viewed as outdated or inefficient, are being re-evaluated not for their convenience, but for their capacity to preserve autonomy. Cash, paper identity, and offline spaces are not simply relics of the pre-digital age; they are quickly becoming the final frontiers of resistance against pervasive datafication. They offer no updates, no analytics, and no APIs. And that is precisely their value. In a time when every transaction, movement, and interaction can be tracked, archived, and analysed, maintaining zones of unobserved life is not regressive—it is strategic.

The global push towards digital-first infrastructure is framed as modernisation. Governments and corporations alike champion digital identity, mobile payments, and online verification as tools for inclusion, transparency, and economic efficiency. And yet, the design of these systems often embeds asymmetries of access and control. A digital identity system may open doors, but it can also lock them. A biometric database may streamline welfare distribution, but it can also exclude those who refuse to submit to scanning. A contactless payment terminal is seamless only if one has a bank account, a stable network connection, and the trust of the financial system. *The absence of analog alternatives transforms inclusion into dependence.*

Resistance to these systems is often mischaracterised as anti-progress or technophobic. But a more honest assessment reveals a deeper logic: it is not the rejection of technology, but the defence of *choice*. Across geographies, communities are asserting the right to operate outside digital systems—not because they are unaware of the benefits, but because they are acutely aware of the risks. They are resisting not the tool, but the centralisation, standardisation, and surveillance that so often accompany it.

Consider the global effort to preserve cash. Sweden's steady march toward a cashless society—where shops, buses, and even churches reject physical currency—has prompted rare pushback from civil rights groups, the elderly, and rural communities. In 2018, the Swedish Civil Contingencies Agency warned that a fully digital economy could make the nation vulnerable to cyberattacks, banking failures, and political coercion. The country's central bank intervened, pressing for legislative protections to guarantee access to cash. What began as a logistical issue evolved into a national debate on resilience and democratic infrastructure. *Cash is not merely a payment method—it is a distributed system of trust that functions without a central switch.*

In Japan, a nation with a robust technological base, cash continues to dominate daily transactions. This is not due to a lack of innovation, but a cultural insistence on privacy and independence. Japanese citizens can conduct their financial affairs without generating a transactional history tied to a mobile number or digital profile. The same is true in Germany, where data protection laws are among the strictest in Europe and cash remains popular. These societies are not lagging; they are choosing. Their analog habits reflect a measured refusal to surrender control over intimate, everyday exchanges.

The preservation of paper identity documents operates on similar logic. Digital ID schemes, from India's Aadhaar to Nigeria's NIN, are often introduced as instruments of inclusion. But their implementation reveals a different story. Aadhaar, the world's largest biometric ID system, has been plagued by data leaks, authentication failures, and access barriers. Welfare recipients have been denied food rations due to fingerprint mismatches or server outages. Elderly citizens have died waiting for pensions that could not be verified by scanners. The system's proponents point to efficiency. Critics point to the bodies.

In contrast, paper IDs—issued locally, verified visually, and held physically—offer a form of authentication that does not depend on electricity, networks, or third-party servers. They can be forged, yes. But they also resist mass profiling, remote deactivation, and centralised blacklisting. *They preserve not only access, but dignity.* For many indigenous communities, retaining control over the mode of identification is not a technological preference but a political imperative. In Canada, some First Nations members have resisted national digital ID programs, opting instead to maintain band-issued identity cards that reflect community governance, not federal classification.

Offline spaces—the physical, unmonitored, and unplugged—represent perhaps the most profound analog sanctuary. Libraries, community centres, public parks, and traditional marketplaces are not simply cultural relics; they are democratic environments where people can gather, speak, and act without being catalogued. In recent years, grassroots groups have deliberately created offline zones, faraday tents, and "no-phone meetings" to reclaim attention, presence, and deliberative space. In these contexts, *resistance takes the form of intentional presence*, a decision not to outsource memory, negotiation, or visibility to digital platforms.

In Oaxaca, Mexico, the indigenous Zapotec community of Guelatao developed its own autonomous mobile network, bypassing national telecoms. The system, maintained by local engineers and paid for collectively, allows calls within the village at no cost and links to external networks at low rates. It's not an act of rebellion; it's a rational design tailored to local needs. Yet it offers a powerful precedent: a communications infrastructure that is not extractive, not surveilled, and not standardised. *It is not merely offline; it is self-determined.*

Even within urbanised, hyperconnected societies, micro-resistances to digital saturation are emerging. The "Right to Disconnect" movement in France, enshrined in labour law, acknowledges that 24/7 connectivity is not a virtue, but a vulnerability. In New York, activists created "zombie phone booths" that mimic functioning payphones but house encrypted offline archives or local community messages. In Barcelona, residents use mesh networks—peer-to-peer WiFi systems—to communicate without relying on corporate ISPs. These examples are not nostalgic—they are tactical. They use analog methods to interrupt the default flow of digital data.

To be clear, analog resistance is not about rejecting technology wholesale. It is about retaining *proportionality*. It is about ensuring that when systems fail—or are misused, censored, or weaponised—alternatives exist. It is about creating redundancy, not dependency. As governments increasingly link welfare benefits to biometric ID, and as corporations move to eliminate cash from storefronts, analog options are not just desirable—they are essential to preserving equity. *Without them, participation becomes conditional on compliance.*

There are tensions, of course. Analog systems can be inefficient, more vulnerable to fraud, and less scalable. But these trade-offs must be understood in context. Speed and convenience are not universal priorities. For someone in a rural area with limited connectivity, a paper form may be more accessible than a digital portal. For someone escaping domestic violence, using cash may offer safety that a debit card cannot. For someone undocumented, the lack of a national ID may be the only thing preventing detention. *Analog systems create friction—but sometimes, friction protects.*

Crucially, analog sanctuaries remind us that technology is not inevitable. It is always a choice, shaped by values, policies, and design decisions. The push toward digital-first governance assumes that progress means total legibility. But not all human life can—or should—be rendered into machine-readable formats. Silence, ambiguity, anonymity, and refusal are part of a healthy civic fabric. A community that cannot opt out is not included—it is *enclosed.*

For policymakers, the challenge is to resist the binary framing of analog as outdated and digital as enlightened. Real inclusion means supporting both. It means ensuring that a person can pay for groceries in cash, sign a form with a pen, or hold an ID in their hand—without penalty, stigma, or delay. It means preserving paper trails, not just server logs. It means treating analog infrastructure not as a fallback, but as a public good.

Analog sanctuaries are not the past clawing at the future. They are *choices* made by people who refuse to be fully seen, sorted, or simulated. They preserve space for human judgment, mutual trust, and unmonitored action. In doing so, they resist not only surveillance but *standardisation*—the flattening of all difference into data. They remind us that not all value can be measured, and not all identity can be verified. They remind us that sometimes, the most powerful act of resistance is not innovation, but *refusal.*

Counter-Design and Guerrilla Tech

If surveillance is the architecture of control, then counter-design is the blueprint of defiance. Beneath the glossy veneer of smart cities, biometric IDs, and predictive policing lies a parallel world of subversion—quiet, inventive, often improvised. Here, technologists, artists, cryptographers, and ordinary citizens are not just resisting, they are *reprogramming.* They are repurposing the very tools of digital oversight to restore human agency, spoof centralised systems, and carve out spaces for untraceable action. This is not about destruction—it is about reclaiming authorship over systems that were never designed with the public's sovereignty in mind.

The notion that the only response to technological overreach is political protest is outdated. Protest matters—but it is no longer the only, or even the primary, terrain on which resistance unfolds. Today, a growing network of practitioners work at the level of infrastructure itself. They don't chant slogans—they rewrite the code, scramble the signal, and interrupt the flow. What binds them is not ideology but intent: *to expose, confuse, evade, or misdirect systems that assume total legibility*. Theirs is a new kind of activism—one rooted not in visibility, but in friction.

Take the example of adversarial fashion—an unlikely yet effective form of wearable resistance. In response to the proliferation of facial recognition technologies, designers such as Kate Rose and the collective CHBL have developed garments that confuse computer vision systems. Patterned scarves and jackets distort the contours that AI uses to identify faces, rendering wearers invisible to surveillance cameras while remaining unremarkable to human eyes. These designs do not disable the system; they exploit its assumptions. *They reveal that surveillance is not omnipotent—it is brittle, dependent on standardised inputs and predictable behaviours.*

Similarly, community-developed spoofing apps allow users to inject false signals into location-based systems. Projects like Randonautica—originally built as a philosophical exploration of randomness—have been retooled in certain contexts to generate GPS noise, complicating location profiling.

Meanwhile, researchers at the University of Washington demonstrated how ultrasonic tones, inaudible to humans but detectable by smartphones, could be used to manipulate voice assistants without alerting the user. While their purpose was academic, their implications were tactical: *the same systems that record can be made to mishear.*

Encryption, once relegated to niche academic circles, has become a pillar of modern digital resistance. Tools like Signal, Matrix, and Briar offer end-to-end encrypted communication outside the purview of telecom providers and state surveillance. More than secure messaging apps, they represent a rethinking of infrastructure: decentralised, peer-authenticated, and metadata-minimising. But even here, the terrain is contested. Governments in India, the UK, and Brazil have sought to compel companies to introduce backdoors in the name of national security. In this climate, *the choice to use encryption is not just technical—it is political.*

Guerrilla technology goes beyond encryption, however. Consider the proliferation of mesh networks—local, peer-to-peer wireless infrastructures that function independently of the internet. During the Hong Kong protests, demonstrators used apps like Bridgefy and FireChat, which allow smartphones to form localised, decentralised networks via Bluetooth, bypassing cellular infrastructure entirely. These tools became vital as authorities throttled mobile service and tracked digital footprints. *When bandwidth becomes a weapon, resilience looks like proximity.*

Other interventions target data collection at the hardware level. The Raspberry Pi Zero, a cheap, programmable microcontroller, has been used to build mobile devices that can detect nearby Wi-Fi sniffers and signal jammers, enabling activists to map surveillance zones in real time. Tactical Tech, a Berlin-based collective, has created DIY kits that teach users how to assemble tools that expose algorithmic profiling, monitor data leaks, or generate noise within behavioural databases. These kits are not commercial—they are *educational armaments for a digital terrain.*

There is also the strategic use of deception—not to lie, but to flood. Tools like AdNauseam automatically click on every advertisement a user sees, polluting data profiles with noise. The result is a browser history so erratic and incoherent that behavioural predictions become unreliable. Similarly, the "Data Poisoning" movement encourages users to upload deliberately absurd or contradictory information to platforms that aggregate user behaviour. *The goal is not to disappear—but to become illegible.*

Some of the most creative counter-designs emerge from communities not traditionally associated with digital innovation. Indigenous groups in Latin America have adapted mapping tools to document land rights without surrendering geo-coordinates to extractive industries. In the Philippines, journalists under digital attack use typewriters and paper archives to protect whistleblower testimonies. In Detroit, grassroots technologists have launched community Wi-Fi initiatives that avoid corporate ISPs, providing encrypted, locally governed internet access. These are not experiments. They are acts of *territorial sovereignty in the digital domain.*

This form of resistance, however, is not without ethical friction. Spoofing systems can have collateral consequences. Noise can obstruct not only surveillance but also safety. A mesh network can be used for dissent—or disinformation. The line between obfuscation and sabotage is thin, and often context-dependent. The legitimacy of guerrilla tech depends not only on what it disrupts, but how, and why. *In a world of opaque systems, ethics cannot be imposed from above—they must be reasoned from below, case by case, consequence by consequence.*

Furthermore, not all counter-designs are oppositional. Some are restorative. The Free Software Foundation, the Open Source Initiative, and decentralised tech communities continue to build privacy-preserving tools not to attack existing systems, but to offer better ones. Mastodon, for example, is not a "Twitter alternative"—it is a reimagining of what social interaction looks like when federated, non-commercial, and user-controlled. Similarly, the Tails operating system allows journalists, whistleblowers, and dissidents to work safely on any computer without leaving a trace. *These are not tweaks—they are epistemological ruptures with the logic of extraction.*

What distinguishes counter-design from simple tool-making is its intentionality. These technologies are not just built—they are *aimed.* They ask: what if systems were designed to *protect the user rather than profile them*? What if surveillance was not a default, but an aberration? What if anonymity was not treated as a crime, but a right? These are not utopian dreams—they are design briefs, coded into libraries, hashed into protocols, embedded in firmware.

Still, challenges remain. Many counter-surveillance tools remain inaccessible to non-technical users. Usability often lags behind innovation. The open-source community, for all its brilliance, struggles with sustainability and scale. Meanwhile, commercial platforms exploit the convenience of defaults to maintain dominance. *To resist effectively, counter-design must not only work—it must be desirable, habitual, and teachable.*

Educational initiatives are vital. The rise of digital literacy bootcamps, cryptoparties, and privacy toolkits represents a cultural shift—towards informed refusal. These are not tutorials; they are rites of passage into a new digital consciousness. They invite users to see themselves not as consumers of tech, but *as co-authors of its terms.* Teaching someone to use Tor is not just a skill transfer—it is a political awakening.

Ultimately, counter-design and guerrilla tech remind us that every system is made—and therefore can be unmade or reimagined. No architecture is too monolithic to be disrupted from below. No protocol is beyond reinterpretation. *The goal is not to destroy infrastructure but to decentralise authorship, to restore interpretive power to those who live within these systems.*

What began as reactive—scrambling signals, spoofing trackers—has matured into a philosophy of creation: *to build technologies that decentralise power, foreground consent, and centre human dignity.* This is not innovation for its own sake. It is insurgent engineering. It is solidarity encoded. And in the face of invisible empires built on data, it may be one of the last defences that does not merely protest—but redesigns the rules entirely.

The Ethics of Obstruction

There are moments when compliance becomes complicity. When participation in a system designed for control is no longer neutral, but an endorsement of its legitimacy. In such moments, refusal—carefully considered, ethically grounded refusal—can be one of the most profound expressions of responsibility. Yet the moral terrain of obstruction is fraught. When is it right to withhold consent, to mislead, to sabotage? At what point does resistance cross into recklessness? These questions are no longer theoretical. As digital control systems become more integrated into daily life, the decision to opt out, distort, or disobey is not merely personal—it is political, and increasingly, moral.

Modern systems of control are rarely enforced by brute coercion alone. They are engineered for smoothness, designed to secure compliance through default settings, not force. A person can passively enable surveillance, tracking, profiling, even discrimination—simply by using a phone, clicking 'I agree,' or scanning a QR code. In such a context, *doing nothing is doing something.* The problem is that those who seek to resist these systems often find that there are few legitimate avenues to challenge them. Opt-out clauses are cosmetic. Appeals are ignored. Alternatives are non-existent. It is in this climate that obstruction gains its ethical weight—not as sabotage for its own sake, but as *the last available mechanism of consent.*

Consider the use of false data as a means of resisting algorithmic profiling. A user deliberately inputs incorrect birthdates, location data, or interests to mislead advertising platforms or facial recognition algorithms. Is this dishonest? Perhaps. But is it unethical? That depends on the nature of the system being manipulated. If the system exists to exploit or commodify identity without meaningful user consent, then the ethics of deception shift. In such cases, *lying to a machine that presumes to know you without permission can be a form of truth-telling.* It restores a fragment of control to a context otherwise devoid of reciprocity.

Similarly, acts of refusal—declining to use biometric authentication, refusing to install mandatory tracking apps, declining digital IDs—can be framed as civil disobedience. These acts rarely come without cost. In India, individuals who declined to link their Aadhaar biometric ID to welfare accounts were denied food rations and pensions. In China, opting out of state apps may mean exclusion from mobility, education, or employment. When refusal is met with exclusion, it reveals that *participation was never freely chosen in the first place.* It was engineered under conditions of duress. Under such circumstances, ethical refusal is not sabotage—it is self-preservation.

Yet the moral case for obstruction is not uniform. Not all resistance is responsible. Actions that produce collateral harm—crashing systems used by hospitals, spreading disinformation under the guise of protest, or compromising third-party data—demand greater scrutiny. The legitimacy of obstruction depends not only on the intent behind it but the *precision of its targeting.* Ethical sabotage is scalpel, not sledgehammer.

Whistleblowing represents a different kind of obstruction—one that exposes the inner workings of oppressive systems to public scrutiny. When Chelsea Manning leaked US military documents, or when Edward Snowden revealed mass surveillance by the NSA, the public learned what had been hidden behind secrecy and plausible deniability. Critics accused both of endangering national security. Supporters viewed them as truth-tellers, compelled by conscience. What makes whistleblowing ethically potent is that it sacrifices personal safety for public knowledge. *It converts private moral clarity into collective ethical opportunity.* In doing so, it sharpens public debate and challenges institutional impunity.

But obstruction need not be dramatic to be moral. Sometimes, it is the small acts that carry the most subversive weight. A developer inserting code that disables tracking functions by default. A teacher explaining how to bypass school surveillance software. A designer building friction into an app to slow addictive use. These are not accidents; they are quiet forms of defiance, rooted in professional integrity. *They are acts of conscience embedded in design.*

Obstruction also arises when systems of control co-opt humanitarian language. Programmes pitched as 'digital inclusion,' 'smart governance,' or 'public safety' often mask intrusive monitoring, data extraction, or behavioural engineering. In such cases, the ethical burden shifts. If a programme claims to uplift but operates through coercion, then undermining it—through exposure, non-participation, or technical disruption—can be an act of moral clarity. This is particularly true when those affected have no genuine voice in the system's design. *Ethical obstruction is most justified when it speaks on behalf of those denied representation.*

However, even justified resistance must grapple with strategic limits. If every system is obstructed, does functionality collapse? Do we risk undermining collective goods, like public health or infrastructure stability? These are not abstract hypotheticals. During the COVID-19 pandemic, opposition to digital contact tracing apps emerged from both privacy advocates and conspiracy theorists. Some objections were grounded in valid concerns over data retention, state overreach, or lack of transparency. Others veered into denialism. The challenge is to *differentiate ethical refusal from ideological sabotage.* Resistance must be guided not only by what it opposes, but what it seeks to preserve.

This tension surfaces acutely in environments where trust in institutions has eroded. In such settings, obstructing digital systems may be less about a principled stand and more about survival. Refugees who avoid biometric registration out of fear their data will be shared with hostile regimes are not engaging in sabotage—they are enacting self-defence. Communities that protect their spaces from digital mapping to prevent resource exploitation are not anti-progress—they are asserting land sovereignty. *Obstruction, in these cases, is not an abstraction. It is a lived necessity.*

There is also a generational dimension to the ethics of obstruction. Younger technologists, particularly in open-source and decentralised communities, often operate under a different moral logic than the corporate environments from which they emerge. For them, the legitimacy of a system is not assumed—it must be earned. If a platform monetises user attention without consent, distorts discourse through opaque algorithms, or compromises safety in pursuit of engagement, then working against it is not sabotage—it is *a recalibration of values.* Resistance becomes design by other means.

Nevertheless, as digital infrastructure becomes increasingly centralised and globally integrated, the space for ethical obstruction narrows. Legal regimes criminalise encryption, mandate biometric compliance, and penalise circumvention. Many forms of resistance that were once legal—anonymous browsing, metadata masking, using false names—are being reframed as threats. The result is that *morality and legality are diverging at scale*. Ethics no longer flows from law—it precedes it.

This divergence creates a new responsibility for individuals and institutions alike. Developers must think not only about what they *can* build, but what they *should*. Users must assess not just what systems *offer*, but what they *demand in return*. Activists must calculate not only impact, but risk. And policymakers must contend with a world in which disobedience is not always dysfunction—but sometimes *the final expression of dignity*.

Ultimately, the ethics of obstruction is not a settled doctrine—it is a dynamic field of judgment. It requires context, discernment, and a willingness to confront uncomfortable truths: that many systems presented as neutral are not; that trust is not owed but earned; and that obedience, in certain cases, can be the greater moral failing. *Obstruction, when disciplined, targeted, and transparent, is not the opposite of order—it is its necessary audit.*

In a world increasingly governed by systems that prioritise efficiency over fairness, prediction over consent, and compliance over understanding, the act of saying no—carefully, strategically, and with moral clarity—remains one of the few tools left to remind those systems that they are neither natural nor inevitable. They are made. And what is made can still be contested.

Chapter 9

Reclaiming the Right to Be Unmeasured

The most radical act of resistance today may be this: *to remain unknown.* In a culture that assigns value through metrics, visibility, and digital legibility, choosing to be unmeasured is not passivity—it is power reclaimed. The systems shaping modern life increasingly demand exposure in exchange for participation. Apps count our steps, platforms analyse our speech, wearables track our sleep. Governments register our irises, retailers trace our gestures, employers monitor our keystrokes. Surveillance is no longer limited to security—it is embedded in convenience, marketed as personalisation, and disguised as progress. But what if this project of endless measurement is not neutral? What if it is *eroding the very conditions of being human*?

This chapter begins with a proposition that runs counter to dominant narratives of innovation: *not all that is counted counts, and not all that counts can—or should—be counted.* The right to be unmeasured is not an argument for regression or digital abstinence. It is a call to re-centre human dignity in systems that increasingly reduce people to data. It is a refusal to accept that value must be validated by an algorithm, or that relevance is determined by analytics dashboards. At stake is more than privacy; it is the architecture of selfhood.

The chapters before this have explored how infrastructures of control operate through coercion, nudging, compliance, and fear. This one turns to what is often missing from those discussions: *interiority*—the protected, ambiguous, private space within a person that is beyond reach. This space is not merely sentimental; it is strategic. It is the zone in which moral judgment is exercised, creativity emerges, dissent is incubated, and authentic freedom is cultivated. When every preference is predicted and every choice pre-optimised, the sovereign mind becomes rare. This is not accidental. The more measured a person becomes, the more manipulable they become. Systems of control do not just restrict movement or speech—they shape what people *desire.* To reclaim the right to be unmeasured, then, is to reclaim the right to *want differently*.

The architecture of the quantified self was built on a seductive promise: that through tracking and feedback, one could achieve greater awareness, efficiency, even transcendence. But in practice, many have found that such systems often displace, rather than enhance, agency. A person who relies on a smartwatch to tell them when to stand, or an app to tell them how to breathe, may gradually outsource intuition, judgment, and even bodily knowledge. This is not awareness—it is *delegated cognition*. And it has a cost. Studies in behavioural psychology have shown that when individuals are constantly evaluated, they become more risk-averse, more conformist, and less creative. Over time, the need to appear optimised overtakes the freedom to be complex.

This is not a rejection of technology—it is a challenge to its framing. Digitisation is often equated with progress, but *progress for whom, and at what cost?* If a system increases efficiency but reduces trust, if it expands access but erodes autonomy, is it truly progressive? The metrics of success used to justify such systems rarely include the unquantifiable: psychological safety, cultural integrity, spiritual fulfilment, or mutual care. When public discourse is structured around data points and performance indicators, these dimensions are not just ignored—they are rendered unintelligible. What cannot be measured is assumed not to exist.

It is here that alternative design becomes not only possible, but imperative. Throughout this chapter, we will explore communities, tools, and practices that resist this flattening. From cash economies that preserve anonymity, to identity systems that prioritise consent over extraction, to civic technologies that foreground relational trust rather than compliance—there is a growing ecosystem of efforts to *design for dignity*. These are not nostalgic retreats into the past; they are forward-looking efforts to embed ethics into infrastructure. Their value lies not in what they quantify, but in what they deliberately leave unmeasured.

Indigenous communities have long modelled systems of knowledge and governance that defy digitised categorisation. Oral traditions, communal land use, non-linear time—all challenge the assumption that data capture is the only valid means of recording reality. In many such communities, privacy is not a technical configuration; it is a social norm, maintained through trust and reciprocity. These practices are not primitive—they are resilient. In fact, they may offer a vocabulary for what it means to be free *within* community, not *from* it.

In resisting quantification, we are also invited to reconsider what it means to be seen. Visibility in digital systems is often confused with affirmation. But being seen by a platform is not the same as being understood by a person. It may mean surveillance, profiling, and instrumentalisation. To *not* be seen, in such a context, is not marginalisation—it can be a form of sanctuary. This is especially true for those whose identities are regularly misread, misclassified, or weaponised by automated systems. To withdraw from the gaze of machines can be an act of self-defence—and, sometimes, of solidarity.

The cultural valorisation of measurement has also shaped how we relate to time. Productivity apps, task trackers, and life-logging tools convert the fluidity of experience into units of output. Rest is only justified if it improves performance. Relationships are nurtured through platforms that assign numerical value to connection. Even leisure becomes content. Against this backdrop, the unmeasured life is more than a rebellion—it is a recovery. *To live without being monitored is not to disappear; it is to reappear to oneself.*

This chapter will close not with solutions, but with an invitation: to imagine a life not structured by metrics, targets, or scores, but by meaning. A life in which one's worth is not defined by data trails or algorithmic relevance. A life in which mystery is not a threat, but a gift. This is not a naive proposition. It is a moral one. And it begins not with a change in technology, but with a change in belief: *that we are more than what we reveal, and that the parts we keep private are not defects—but sites of possibility.*

Reclaiming the right to be unmeasured does not mean rejecting all systems of order or abandoning shared metrics where they serve genuine communal aims. It means restoring the balance between knowing and not knowing, between revealing and withholding, between participating and opting out. It requires recognising that control is not always imposed—it is also invited, through habits of convenience, and surrendered, one click at a time.

The unquantified life is not an escape. It is a stance. One that says: *I will not be defined by your dashboard. I am not your input. I am not your outcome. I am not your data.* In this refusal, something new begins—not a system, not a platform, but a practice of remembering what it means to be human before becoming measurable.

The Sovereign Mind

There is a quiet dignity in not being seen. A strength in being unreadable. A form of sovereignty that does not announce itself through metrics, performance, or algorithmic fluency—but through restraint, silence, and self-containment. In a cultural moment obsessed with self-disclosure, optimisation, and behavioural transparency, the decision to remain opaque becomes an act of principled resistance. Not because one has something to hide, but because one understands that some things are worth keeping untouched by the grasp of systems.

The sovereign mind is not a fantasy of independence; it is a cultivated state of interior freedom. It begins with the right to retreat—not as escapism, but as a prerequisite for discernment. It values ambiguity not as a defect of knowledge, but as a shelter for depth. It does not chase constant input, nor outsource its instincts to the feedback loops of social platforms or the nudges of predictive algorithms. Instead, it builds the capacity to dwell in its own presence without mediation, surveillance, or validation. *Privacy, in this sense, is not the mere absence of exposure—it is the condition for wholeness.*

For systems of control to function, they require visibility. Visibility is the terrain of legibility, standardisation, and ultimately, regulation. What is seen can be categorised. What is categorised can be ranked, sorted, or governed. And what is governed, in digital terms, can be nudged, profiled, or denied. The sovereign mind defies this sequence—not by confronting it head-on at every instance, but by choosing when and where to show up. It is a refusal to be always on, always trackable, always known. It does not consent to be flattened into a data point.

This refusal is neither antisocial nor technophobic. It is strategic. It is about reclaiming cognitive agency in environments where attention has become a commodity and where identity is increasingly defined by externally verifiable interactions. Consider how the most intimate parts of a person's inner life—preferences, memories, moods, even moments of grief or arousal—are now potential metadata. A fitness tracker can detect sadness. A voice assistant can register tension. A recommendation algorithm can know your cravings before you name them. In such a world, *the decision to hold something privately, unrecorded and unshared, becomes an act of protecting not just privacy, but personhood itself.*

One of the more pernicious features of surveillance culture is how it normalises the outsourcing of inner judgment. Whether it's deferring to

Google Maps for every decision of direction, to a rating system before trying a new experience, or to a calendar notification to tell us when to breathe—each moment of external reliance, though trivial in isolation, can accumulate into a pattern of learned dependence. It's not the tools that erode autonomy; it's the dulling of discernment that occurs when we stop noticing we've surrendered choice.

This atrophy of internal life is rarely intentional. It's an ambient process. It happens when interfaces are designed to be frictionless, when convenience is elevated as the highest value, and when the self becomes a manager of its own digital representation rather than an integrated whole. The sovereign mind resists that trend not by disengaging from technology entirely, but by remaining alert to where and how it cedes authority. It asks: *Is this choice truly mine? Is this reaction cultivated, or conditioned? Am I operating from presence or programming?*

To foster a sovereign mind requires both discipline and a re-evaluation of what constitutes intelligence. In institutional settings—schools, workplaces, even government policy—measurable intelligence is often prioritised. Standardised test scores, productivity metrics, psychometric assessments. What's harder to capture, and therefore often ignored, is interiority: reflection, emotional range, intuitive synthesis, moral imagination. A system that cannot measure a trait will eventually devalue it. But *what cannot be measured is often what anchors our humanity.*

Ambiguity, for instance, is not confusion. It is the ability to hold multiple possibilities without rushing toward binary closure. It is vital for ethical reasoning, for empathy, for navigating complexity. Yet in algorithmic culture, ambiguity is a bug to be resolved. Uncertainty must be converted into preference. Indecision must be pathologised as inefficiency. The sovereign mind cultivates the capacity to pause within ambiguity—not as a delay, but as an inquiry. *It knows that some truths emerge only when space is made for them to arrive unforced.*

Similarly, silence is not the absence of communication. It is a modality of awareness that exceeds language. A person who never experiences silence—literal or mental—is a person who cannot distinguish their own thoughts from the noise of the world. Modern digital life, with its unending prompts, scrolls, pings, and suggestions, actively undermines silence. It makes boredom intolerable and solitude suspect. But without silence, we cannot think originally. We cannot attune to intuition. We cannot hear the whisper of conscience over the roar of metrics.

This chapter is an invitation to reclaim that interior space—not as a luxury, but as a necessity for ethical life. And it begins by reorienting one's attention from what is being broadcast about oneself to what is being experienced within. That turn inward is not narcissism. It is the condition for moral clarity. *Only a mind that is not constantly being shaped by external signals can recognise when those signals are manipulative, coercive, or dehumanising.*

Practically, this might involve opting out of platforms designed to extract data. It might mean cultivating media hygiene, choosing not to participate in oversharing culture, or simply setting boundaries around what parts of the self are offered up for digital validation. But the deeper act is internal. It is the quiet reassertion of authorship over one's inner life. It is the decision to be incompletely known to the system, and wholly known to oneself.

This is not a nostalgic call to return to a pre-digital world. It is a strategic call to reframe what we consider valuable. In a world obsessed with quantification, the sovereign mind does not reject technology, but *chooses how to engage with it on its own terms.* It knows when to step back. When not to respond. When to resist being interpreted.

Reflection prompts at the end of this section are not exercises in performance but in realignment. They are not for display. They are not for optimisation. They are for one person alone: the reader. That too is part of sovereignty—restoring experiences that are not meant to be shared, but cherished. Unmeasured. Unrecorded. Undisturbed.

Because some parts of us do not need to be improved, tracked, or translated. They need to be left alone. Not because they are weak or broken—but because they are sacred. And that, perhaps, is the most radical act left: *to live some part of life off the record—not as retreat, but as a form of resistance, and ultimately, of reclamation.*

Rethinking Progress

It is one of the most enduring assumptions of modern governance, corporate policy, and development thinking: that digitisation equals progress. Faster processing, real-time analytics, frictionless transactions, cloud-based identity, algorithmic decision-making—all wrapped in the language of innovation, inclusion, and efficiency. To question this trajectory is often framed as retrograde, out-of-touch, or anti-technology. But if one sets aside the marketing gloss and examines the lived consequences of digital systems—especially in domains such as education, health, public services, and financial access—a more complicated picture emerges. *Not all that is digital is dignified. Not all that is optimised is humane.*

Progress is not a neutral term. It is directional, implying not just change but improvement—an ascent toward something more refined, more evolved. When digitisation becomes the default benchmark of progress, the risk is that other values—human judgement, trust, slowness, confidentiality, consent—are quietly sacrificed in the name of technological inevitability. This is not a critique of technology itself, but a call to interrogate the *frameworks* through which we evaluate it. What would it mean to centre dignity—not efficiency—as the axis of technological appraisal?

The case for digital transformation is often persuasive on the surface. Governments digitise welfare systems to reduce fraud and speed up delivery. Banks shift to online platforms for convenience and cost savings. Schools adopt learning management systems to personalise education and track performance. And yet, beneath these surface improvements lies a deeper shift in power. When a service goes digital, it typically introduces layers of surveillance, conditions of access, and systemic opacity that did not previously exist. If an individual does not have the requisite device, connectivity, literacy, or biometric data, they are not just inconvenienced—they are excluded entirely. *Efficiency without accessibility is not progress. It is segmentation.*

India's Aadhaar project is often presented as a triumph of digital public infrastructure: a biometric identity system covering over a billion citizens, enabling everything from food rations to mobile SIM activation. But the very same system has documented cases where elderly individuals were denied rations due to fingerprint mismatch, or where system outages blocked pension disbursements. These are not technical glitches—they are moral failures. They reveal a design logic that prioritises systemic throughput over individual dignity. If the efficiency of a system is predicated on treating exceptions as expendable, *then the system itself is ethically defective, regardless of how advanced its architecture may be.*

There is also the question of *consent.* Most digital infrastructures operate under a logic of asymmetry. Individuals must comply, often blindly, with terms of service they cannot reasonably contest. Opt-out mechanisms are rare, and when they exist, they are functionally meaningless for anyone dependent on state services, employment, or digital identity. Surveillance is embedded by default—location tracking, behavioural analytics, facial recognition—all with the veneer of improving user experience or reducing administrative overhead. Yet there is no real parity between user and system. *A coerced transaction does not become consensual simply because it occurred through an app.*

The framing of efficiency itself deserves scrutiny. Efficiency, as commonly defined in tech circles, means reducing friction, speeding throughput, and lowering costs. But these goals often neglect qualitative dimensions of human interaction—time for deliberation, space for dissent, nuance in communication. A system optimised for metrics can misread needs entirely. For example, a chatbot might efficiently process customer complaints but completely fail to capture distress, urgency, or cultural nuance. A predictive policing algorithm might optimise patrol routes based on crime statistics, yet entrench racial profiling in the process. *When metrics become proxies for meaning, dignity becomes a casualty.*

Dignity, by contrast, demands slower, more relational ways of evaluating technology. It considers whether a system enables participation without coercion. Whether it respects cognitive diversity and allows for ambiguity. Whether it can accommodate human error without punishment. Whether its benefits are distributed equitably, rather than reinforcing existing asymmetries. Crucially, it asks whether individuals can *refuse* participation without disproportionate penalty. A system that cannot tolerate refusal is not serving people—it is disciplining them.

This shift in evaluative lens has implications far beyond policy design. It touches product development, UX design, regulatory frameworks, and even ethics education in engineering curricula. The question is not just *what does the technology do*, but *what kind of world does it assume and reinforce*? Does it presume constant connectivity as a norm, thereby penalising those in rural or under-resourced areas? Does it assume data-sharing as a default social good, thereby eroding the very concept of personal sovereignty? Does it treat outliers as friction, or as legitimate ends in themselves?

One illustrative case is Estonia, often celebrated for its e-governance infrastructure. Nearly every public service can be accessed digitally—taxes, voting, prescriptions, school enrolment. For many, this model is aspirational. But even in Estonia, maintaining analog options for certain services remains important—not just as redundancy, but as a recognition that not all citizens navigate systems in the same way. The choice to accommodate variance is a subtle but profound act of dignity. It communicates that *citizens are not units to be processed, but individuals to be engaged.*

Similarly, the use of blockchain for land titling in Honduras and Ghana was initially promoted as a means to bring clarity and reduce corruption. Yet when mapped onto local realities—communal land ownership, low digital literacy, minimal infrastructure—the same systems could produce confusion, fraud, and alienation. Again, the issue is not with the technology itself, but with the mismatch between technical assumptions and human contexts. *A dignified system does not just work flawlessly in code; it works meaningfully in people's lives.*

To be clear, there are areas where digitisation has indeed enhanced dignity. Text-to-speech tools for the visually impaired. Secure messaging apps for activists. Crisis response tools that coordinate relief with unprecedented speed. These are not trivial gains. But they stand out because they are designed *with and for* the affected populations—not imposed upon them as part of an abstract innovation agenda. They respect difference. They accommodate refusal. They operate with the humility that *not everything that can be digitised should be.*

What, then, would a framework for dignity-centred technology evaluation look like? At minimum, it would include the following questions: Does the system permit opt-out without penalty? Does it offer transparency and explainability at the point of interaction? Can it accommodate edge cases without causing harm? Is its value defined primarily in human terms—not just time saved or costs reduced, but agency preserved, care extended, relationships strengthened? And finally, *does the system serve the user, or does the user exist to feed the system?*

This is not a semantic debate. The answers to these questions determine the structure of social trust. A society where people feel surveilled, coerced, and reduced to behavioural profiles is one in which civic life frays. But a society that prioritises dignity—where people can choose, refuse, err, and be heard—is one where technology can genuinely serve progress. Not because it is frictionless, but because it is human.

The point is not to romanticise slowness or fetishise the analog. Nor is it to deny the immense potential of digital systems in domains like medicine, climate modelling, or disaster preparedness. Rather, it is to insist that *progress must be interrogated through the lens of human flourishing.* Not just GDP growth or institutional efficiency, but whether people feel respected, recognised, and free.

We must learn to ask of every system: What does it ask of us? What does it cost us in mental energy, in relational trust, in psychic sovereignty? Does it allow room for interpretation, or does it narrow us into inputs? Does it encourage reflection, or reflex? Does it make us more human, or more predictable?

Until these questions are embedded in our conception of progress, we risk mistaking acceleration for advancement. And the faster we move without them, the more likely we are to build systems that forget whom they were meant to serve in the first place. Progress, if it is to be worthy of the name, must always be checked against *dignity, diversity, and the irreducible mystery of being human.*

"Designing for Dignity."

The dominant ethos shaping digital systems today—whether financial platforms, welfare delivery mechanisms, or smart city infrastructure—tends to valorise efficiency, scalability, and data extraction above all else. Functionality is engineered for frictionless compliance, not consent. Human beings become mere variables in a statistical model, reduced to risk profiles, user metrics, or compliance scores. Dignity, when it appears in this landscape, is ornamental—a marketing layer draped over systems built to monitor, sort, and optimise populations. Yet if we invert this logic and begin not with the system but with the person, what might emerge is a radically different kind of design philosophy: one that recognises human agency as foundational rather than incidental. Designing for dignity is not a utopian indulgence; it is a grounded, pragmatic response to the moral and social distortions embedded in surveillance-driven infrastructures.

At its core, dignity-centred design refuses to accept that control is the price of order. It challenges the idea that trust must be automated, that safety must be datafied, or that fairness can be outsourced to an algorithm. Instead, it prioritises context over prediction, relationships over metrics, and moral complexity over computational neatness. Dignity is not simply about being treated well by systems—it is about having meaningful participation in how those systems are conceived, implemented, and governed. In practice, this means giving communities the power to say not just "yes" or "no," but to shape the very questions being asked.

Consider the design of identity systems. The dominant model—whether Aadhaar in India, ID4D in Africa, or Real ID in the United States—relies on biometric verification, centralised registries, and algorithmic risk scoring. These systems often frame themselves as empowering, offering "legal identity for all," but the underlying architecture is geared toward surveillance and control. Participation may be framed as voluntary, but for millions, refusal results in exclusion from healthcare, education, or income. Alternative models—such as self-sovereign identity or community-issued credentials—prioritise autonomy, selective disclosure, and revocability.

They do not treat the human being as a problem to be solved by a state-backed hash or facial recognition scan, but as a stakeholder with the right to opt out, negotiate terms, or remain unreadable to systems that do not serve them.

The implications of dignity-centred design extend beyond digital ID. In public health, for instance, app-based contact tracing during pandemics was often implemented with little regard for consent, transparency, or decentralisation. Some jurisdictions adopted decentralised privacy-preserving models—like those based on DP-3T protocols—but most leaned towards centralised data collection, citing expediency. Here again, the metric of success was often uptake and coverage, not informed engagement or long-term social trust. Designing for dignity would ask different questions: Who controls the data flow? Is consent truly reversible? Does the system amplify existing inequities, or mitigate them?

In welfare systems, behavioural nudges and algorithmic eligibility scoring have become embedded into the fabric of service delivery. Claimants are increasingly subject to opaque risk assessments, automated sanctions, and nudging mechanisms designed to "optimise behaviour." These are not neutral tools—they carry implicit value judgements about what constitutes a responsible life. Dignity-centred alternatives would involve co-designed eligibility criteria, real human adjudication, and the right to understand and challenge the rules by which one is governed. The goal is not to optimise citizens for systems, but to build systems that can adapt to the lived realities of citizens.

There are precedents. In Barcelona, the DECODE project allowed residents to decide who could access their personal data and for what purpose. Rather than harvesting behavioural data by default, the system flipped the script: privacy and consent were not opt-outs, but design defaults. In Kenya, M-KOPA's pay-as-you-go solar energy programme faced backlash when its business model led to data-fuelled repossession and over-surveillance of poor households. In response, activists and technologists began developing cooperative energy models that embedded local governance into the tech stack. These examples may seem modest, but they demonstrate a principle: that dignity can be engineered into systems when people—not metrics—are treated as the primary unit of design.

Dignity-centred design also redefines the role of expertise. Traditional development or innovation paradigms often marginalise lived knowledge, treating communities as passive recipients of "solutions" devised elsewhere. A dignity framework insists on reciprocal learning: engineers, designers, and policymakers must be willing to be reshaped by the communities they aim to serve. This is not mere consultation—it is shared authorship. It demands a humility that is rare in the worlds of digital transformation and "scaling up," where impact is too often measured in adoption rates and efficiency gains rather than human flourishing.

Another key element is the relationship between technology and time. Surveillance systems are designed for immediacy: real-time data flows, instant scoring, predictive analytics. But dignity often requires slowness. The ability to pause, reflect, and remain undecided is a form of agency that does not fit easily into systems built for constant monitoring. Consider dispute resolution mechanisms: a human adjudicator can recognise context, acknowledge past trauma, and weigh competing moral claims. An algorithm cannot. Designing for dignity means recognising that some decisions cannot—and should not—be automated.

This shift in design ethos also necessitates new forms of accountability. In dignity-oriented systems, accountability is not satisfied by publishing a transparency report or open-sourcing a machine learning model. It means building mechanisms for redress, reversal, and repair. It means recognising harm not only as a technical failure, but as a relational breach that requires response, not just debugging. It means acknowledging that trust is not a by-product of efficiency, but something that must be cultivated, protected, and—when broken—restored.

Community knowledge plays a central role in these systems. Across indigenous, rural, and grassroots contexts, knowledge is often transmitted through relationship, oral tradition, and collective memory. These are forms of epistemology that are illegible to most digital systems. Designing for dignity does not seek to digitise or extract this knowledge, but to protect the conditions in which it thrives. This may mean refusing to map certain territories, refusing to encode certain rituals, or declining to model behaviour that is deeply contextual. Absence, in this context, is not a bug but a choice.

Relational trust is similarly undervalued in dominant systems. Most digital infrastructures seek to replace trust with verification: trustless systems, zero-knowledge proofs, blockchain consensus mechanisms. While technically elegant, these systems can inadvertently erode the very social fabric they aim to support. When every interaction is mediated by credentials or smart contracts, the need to build human trust diminishes. Designing for dignity restores trust to its rightful place—not as a weakness to be eliminated, but as a strength to be nurtured.

Perhaps most crucially, dignity-centred design affirms the right to opacity. In a culture that prizes transparency, measurability, and performance, the refusal to be captured can be a powerful act. Not every process must be auditable. Not every outcome must be benchmarked. Not every identity must be validated. Systems that honour dignity allow for mystery, ambiguity, and self-definition. They leave space for what is unsaid, unknown, and still becoming. In doing so, they return to a deeper understanding of what it means to be human—not as a data point, but as a subject with agency, memory, and moral depth.

Designing for dignity is not an add-on or afterthought—it is a fundamental reorientation of how we think about systems, relationships, and the role of technology in shaping society. It does not offer a blueprint so much as a set of commitments: to participation over prediction, to care over control, and to people over metrics. It is slow work, quiet work, and at times inconvenient work—but it is necessary if we are to build futures in which human flourishing is not merely a slogan, but a design principle in itself.

The Unquantified Life

It is not merely data we surrender when we allow ourselves to be counted, tracked, and scored—it is narrative space, inner complexity, and the dignity of uncertainty. As the digitised world marches toward total visibility, the cost is not just privacy in the legal sense, but the collapse of that unmeasurable inner frontier where silence once offered sanctuary and contradiction could safely coexist. In the growing pursuit of data as destiny, a life that resists measurement begins to look like an act of quiet rebellion—one grounded not in nostalgia but in principled restraint.

The promise of the quantified self, of devices and dashboards that help us "know ourselves better," rests on a subtle but potent inversion: it implies that what is not measured does not exist, or at least, does not matter. This logic now extends far beyond the consumer wellness industry. It is embedded into policy frameworks, employment systems, insurance algorithms, and educational reform. It governs not just how systems perceive us but increasingly how we perceive ourselves. Metrics replace intuition. Dashboards overrule reflection. And in the name of optimisation, we retreat from ambiguity—the very ground of human freedom.

This is not a call to romanticise the analogue past. It is an appeal to recognise the ideological structure beneath the interface. A fitness tracker may help someone walk more, but it also reshapes what "health" means. A productivity tool may enable more efficient time use, but it also recasts attention as a resource to be extracted. What was once private behaviour becomes a public feed. What was once self-regulated becomes platform-managed. It is not the tool itself that demands scrutiny but the epistemology behind it: that *knowing more* is inherently *knowing better*, and that *better* is universally defined by speed, volume, visibility, and compliance.

Systems of constant measurement do not merely collect data—they condition desire. Surveillance, once understood as the watchful eye of the state, now functions through platforms that invite voluntary exposure. The quantified life thrives on perceived agency: we choose to track, to share, to score. Yet, behind that sense of autonomy lies a deep constraint, engineered subtly through social comparison, institutional reward structures, and behavioural nudges that redefine participation as validation. In such a system, the refusal to measure is misread as failure, inefficiency, or even deviance.

The deeper ethical question is not whether data is being collected responsibly, but whether a world that compels constant accounting can ever preserve dignity. Dignity, in its richest form, is not earned through transparency but through the freedom to hold aspects of one's self and one's life as sacred, incomplete, or unknowable. When every choice becomes a dataset, every action an input, the space for moral and psychological interiority shrinks. The self becomes a product to be monitored rather than a subject to be trusted.

There are historical precedents to this tension. Totalitarian regimes sought control not only through force but through the elimination of ambiguity. The suppression of private thought, informal gathering, and unofficial narrative was not collateral damage; it was the strategy. What makes our current moment distinct is that these controls are being automated and normalised—not as state edicts, but as upgrades. Our lives are not forcibly digitised; they are gently incentivised into data streams under the banner of convenience, safety, and efficiency.

This dynamic is most dangerous where essential services are contingent on digital participation. Consider education platforms that reward students for daily screen compliance, or job markets that penalise those without algorithmic visibility. The person who opts out of being measured—who resists the app, the wearable, the biometric checkpoint—is not merely choosing anonymity; they risk exclusion. Opting out is rarely neutral. In many domains, it has become a kind of economic or social self-sabotage. Thus, the freedom not to be measured is increasingly an illusion for those who cannot afford the consequences.

And yet, opting out remains essential. Not as a technophobic gesture, but as a strategy of reclaiming one's interior world. What if value were defined not by what can be counted but by what resists counting altogether—intimacy, grief, intuition, spiritual doubt, acts of quiet kindness? What if a person's worth was measured not by traceable outputs but by their capacity to act with presence in contexts where metrics offer no guidance?

The insistence on measuring everything blinds institutions to this deeper form of agency. A teacher's impact, for instance, may be most profound in moments that defy rubric. A doctor's wisdom may lie not in the efficiency of throughput but in the courage to pause, to sit with a patient in silence. A policymaker's success might be found not in maximising uptake but in designing spaces for deliberation. *The essence of human wisdom often lies not in the visible action but in the invisible restraint.*

To reclaim the unquantified life is not to reject information—it is to reject the demand that information be the only path to legitimacy. It is to assert that humans are not just consumers, nodes, users, or citizens-in-data, but moral agents with the right to mystery. This claim requires more than language; it requires structural support. Architectural, legal, and digital systems must be reoriented toward preserving ambiguity—not as inefficiency to be solved but as a protected state of being.

There are design frameworks beginning to move in this direction. The notion of "privacy by design" must evolve into "dignity by design"—systems that do not simply minimise harm but actively support non-instrumental values. Consider community currencies that do not track individual spending but foster shared trust. Consider educational models that reward reflective depth over performative productivity. Consider identity frameworks that offer verifiable credentials without surrendering holistic profiles. These are not hypotheticals; they exist in pilot form across civic tech, indigenous governance, and grassroots resistance efforts. But their survival depends on a shift in cultural metric: from "what works" to "what honours."

This shift cannot be legislated from above. It begins in the personal realm—with small but meaningful refusals. Choosing cash over traceable payments. Leaving the phone at home. Listening without recording. Being present without sharing. These are not regressions. They are modern acts of sovereignty.

To imagine the unquantified life is to refuse to let reality be flattened into analytics. It is to insist that *the deepest parts of being human are not data gaps to be filled, but sanctuaries to be defended.* The question is not how much we can measure. It is what we are willing to remain silent about—for the sake of freedom, for the sake of wholeness, for the sake of being human in ways no system can explain.

Conclusion

The Empire Beneath the Interface

The most powerful systems are those we do not see. Not because they are hidden, but because they are normalised—embedded in interfaces we touch daily, transactions we barely notice, and conveniences we rarely question. The control structures of the past wore uniforms, erected fences, passed decrees. Today's architecture of power prefers subtlety. It slides under our fingers, offers a clean design, and speaks in the soft voice of customer service. It asks for consent not through force, but through fatigue. The empire has moved—not into palaces or parliaments, but into platforms, protocols, and databases. It is ambient, ambiently enforced, and increasingly automated.

This chapter is not about sounding an alarm. The alarm has already been ringing for some time. What remains is learning how to hear it—not as panic, but as clarity. By this point in the book, the reader has traced the evolution of currency into control, data into discipline, identity into instrumentation. We've examined how the mechanics of nudging, registration, exclusion, and gamification construct a behavioural cage—one made not of iron bars, but of interfaces that smile. What's left is not a new warning, but a reckoning: to ask what kind of person, and what kind of society, these systems are shaping us to be.

It is tempting to view these developments as technological in nature, as if data collection, algorithmic enforcement, and digital credentialing are simply the neutral outgrowths of innovation. But this is the final illusion worth shattering. These systems are not only designed—they are *designed for.* They serve the interests of institutions that measure stability by compliance, that conflate safety with surveillance, and that prefer metrics to meaning. The software is not apolitical. The architecture is not accidental. The empire beneath the interface is not a glitch—it is the goal.

The closing question is not whether control exists, but whether we have learned to see it. Not in its most overt expressions, but in the quiet agreements we sign without reading, the permissions we grant without considering, and the integrations we accept because *everyone else has*. The challenge now is not to resist every tool, but to *discern*—to develop the reflex of asking who benefits, what is lost, and what is being reshaped in the process.

This final chapter offers no blueprint for revolution. Instead, it invites something both quieter and more radical: a return to discernment. Discernment is not suspicion. It is not cynicism. It is the cultivated ability to distinguish between what is useful and what is coercive, what is offered and what is demanded, what enhances human dignity and what erodes it behind a UX veneer. Discernment does not require technical mastery. It requires moral clarity and the willingness to stop mistaking frictionless design for benevolence.

Consider, for example, the way "consent" is gathered in digital environments. Whether through app permissions, cookie banners, or biometric scans at borders, the ritual is nearly always the same: a veneer of choice masking a single viable path forward. Say yes—or lose access. Say yes—or stay behind. It is the automation of assent, scaled across populations. And yet, because the option is framed as voluntary, it avoids the ethical scrutiny of coercion. *Control works best when it calls itself care.*

Or reflect on the language of personalisation, a term that once meant tailoring experiences to individual preference, but now often means profiling people into pre-set behavioural categories. Your feed is curated, your options sorted, your habits analysed for the sake of optimising engagement. But optimising *for what*? Often for profit, sometimes for prediction, and rarely, if ever, for your flourishing. *Being known by a system is not the same as being understood by it.* And in this confusion, a subtle form of moral outsourcing occurs: we begin to trust that the system knows best, that its path is most efficient, that its prompts are worth obeying.

The antidote to such subtle control is not paranoia—it is perception. To walk awake through a digital world is to notice not just what a system does, but what it *requires* in exchange. This chapter reorients the reader not toward resistance for its own sake, but toward *attentiveness*. Attentiveness to design. To defaults. To what is framed as inevitable. And most importantly, to what these systems make difficult: silence, ambiguity, refusal, solitude, slowness, care without capture.

We now live in an environment where data is not merely collected, but expected. To opt out is treated as eccentric. To remain unreadable is considered suspect. Privacy itself is often framed as something to "earn," rather than a right to retain. This framing is not accidental—it is part of a larger shift where the unmeasured life is increasingly rendered unintelligible to systems of power. Yet what cannot be measured can still be meaningful. What resists capture can still be human.

This final section is not about nostalgia. It does not romanticise the analogue or reject technology wholesale. Instead, it asks a deeper question: *How can technology serve human dignity, rather than subordinate it?* How can systems be designed with moral constraints, not just technical capabilities? And how can individuals cultivate the reflexes—ethical, emotional, and political—to recognise when a tool becomes a leash?

To answer these questions, readers are invited not into resistance movements, but into a form of personal and civic consciousness. The empire beneath the interface will not be dismantled by outrage alone. It will yield, if at all, to those who learn to *see* its contours, its assumptions, and its incentives. This is the work of reclaiming agency—not through force, but through *insight*. Not through slogans, but through the slow, deliberate act of thinking harder about what we use, how we're used, and what it means to remain truly human in an increasingly instrumented world.

There is no perfect toolkit. But there is discernment. And it starts with this: to understand that the interface is not the neutral window it pretends to be. It is a map. It is a mask. And occasionally, it is a mirror. What we do with that awareness—how we change our habits, our expectations, and our systems—is the work of the chapters that follow not in this book, but in the world beyond it.

The final chapter weaves the core ideas

Control today rarely raises its voice. It doesn't need to. Instead of marching in uniform, it whispers through user interfaces. It reassures rather than commands, presents options instead of threats, and embeds itself not in declarations but in defaults. Most people do not feel oppressed; they feel serviced, connected, updated, optimised. But beneath the calm surfaces of digital convenience lies a pattern of extraction, surveillance, and subtle constraint. The structures of power have not vanished; they've migrated. They operate not just through law or violence, but through frictionless design and quiet nudges. This is control as infrastructure—unseen not because it is hidden, but because it is ambient.

This chapter is not a warning; the time for warnings has passed. The goal now is recognition. To grasp that the systems shaping our choices are neither neutral nor accidental, and that their influence is not exercised with obvious hostility, but with studied indifference. Predictive algorithms do not care about your wellbeing. Recommendation engines are not your friends. They are tools of capture, and their efficiency depends on one thing: that you remain unaware of their logic while entrusting them with your preferences, your attention, and eventually, your agency.

Yet none of this is inevitable. That is the critical insight. We are not trapped. We are entangled. And entanglement can be studied, understood, and ultimately loosened. The structures that govern so much of our digital lives—from behavioural scoring to biometric classification, from automated content moderation to data brokerage—depend on our cooperation. Sometimes passive, sometimes enthusiastic, but cooperation nonetheless. The invitation here is to reframe your role: not as a user or consumer, but as a participant whose decisions either reinforce or disrupt the system's grip.

The danger is not merely that people are being watched. It is that they are being conditioned. When metrics replace meaning, when dashboards replace dialogue, and when efficiency replaces empathy, something profound is lost—not only in society, but within the self. Every time a person opts for the convenience of frictionless interaction over deliberation, a muscle of discernment weakens. Every time a trade-off is accepted in the name of customisation or speed, the margin for thought shrinks. And when everything is optimised, tracked, and gamified, we begin to mistake what is measurable for what is meaningful.

To awaken intellectually is one thing. To awaken morally is something else entirely. The difference lies in what you choose to do next. Awareness without action is aesthetic. It flatters the intellect but leaves the infrastructure untouched. The call in this final chapter is to go further—not towards revolution, but towards *discernment*: the cultivated ability to recognise what is happening beneath the surface and to respond with clarity, courage, and care. This is not about adopting a new ideology. It is about reclaiming the mental, emotional, and ethical space to decide how much of yourself you are willing to trade for participation.

Consider the concept of 'care' as it now functions in digital systems. Care is no longer personal; it is procedural. It is expressed in automated reminders, behaviour-modifying incentives, and identity-verifying checks. It speaks the language of protection, but enforces the logic of control. When health systems track you to ensure compliance, when financial services analyse your behaviour to assess risk, or when education platforms shape curricula around engagement metrics, the justification is always safety, improvement, or fairness. But safety without consent, improvement without context, and fairness without transparency become instruments of domination dressed as service.

There is an ethical reckoning at the heart of this. When does design shift from helpful to coercive? When does surveillance stop being preventative and become pre-emptive punishment? When do the nudges become chains? These are not technical questions; they are moral ones. And they demand not blanket resistance, but rigorous discernment: of intent, of effect, and of what is being normalised with each passing upgrade.

This chapter also reframes the notion of resistance. Not as opposition for its own sake, but as the preservation of the human capacity to say no—to delay, to question, to seek context before compliance. Resistance in this sense is not about rejecting technology, but about retaining *judgement* in the presence of it. It is about refusing to let interface design replace deliberative thought. It is about remembering that silence, ambiguity, and slowness are not design flaws in the human condition, but critical features of moral agency.

There is a toolkit here, but not the kind you download. It is not made of apps, plugins, or privacy extensions. It is composed of habits: asking who benefits; refusing urgency when clarity is needed; declining to share when silence is more powerful; and choosing friction when convenience hides cost. These are not technical skills. They are human ones. And they grow sharper when exercised in daily life—whether in how you handle your personal data, how you engage with systems that rate or rank you, or how you navigate environments where everything is monitored and optimised.

This is not a romantic plea for retreat. It is a sober call to stay awake. The systems we live within are not neutral, and they are not static. They evolve in response to what we tolerate, what we reward, and what we ignore. To walk through the world awake is to become a feedback loop of a different kind—one that resists reflex, that slows down manipulation, and that feeds a culture of dignity rather than domination. It begins not with confrontation, but with awareness sharpened into intention.

The most hopeful truth may also be the most confronting: the architecture of control requires our consent—not always explicit, but functional. It requires that we stop asking questions. It requires that we treat metrics as meaning. It requires that we internalise the priorities of the system as if they were our own. And once this is understood, something shifts. The interface is no longer invisible. It becomes legible. The prompt to opt in is recognised as a demand, the default as a decision already made for you.

This is the first step toward reclaiming power—not by dismantling the system overnight, but by navigating it with eyes open.

What you do next matters. Not because you can single-handedly change the system, but because every act of discernment weakens the hold of systems built on invisibility. Every refusal to be reduced to a datapoint, every pause before giving consent, every conversation that exposes the mechanics behind the design—they all contribute to an infrastructure of awareness. And that is where change begins.

The tools of domination have been upgraded. So too must our response. Not with louder outrage, but with deeper clarity. Not with utopian alternatives, but with practical discernment. Not with the illusion that we are free, but with the conviction that freedom begins the moment we stop mistaking smooth experiences for ethical ones. The empire beneath the interface thrives on passivity. Discernment disrupts it—not with noise, but with knowing.

About the Author

Arun Thorne writes at the intersection of power, technology, and the human condition. With a background spanning policy analysis, digital ethics, and systems design, his work explores how modern societies shape—and are shaped by—the tools they build. He has spent over a decade studying how identity, data, and currency are quietly transformed into instruments of governance. His writing is driven by a singular mission: to help people see what is hidden in plain sight. Arun lives between cities and silence, often off-grid, always observing. Economies of Control is his most urgent work to date—a map for those who refuse to sleepwalk into the future.

www.ingramcontent.com/pod-product-compliance
Lightning Source LLC
Chambersburg PA
CBHW061609180926
51615CB00006B/25
* 9 7 8 8 1 9 9 1 1 7 9 1 4 *